PORTS OF ENTRY
Ethnic Impressions

ABELLE MASON

PORTS OF ENTRY
Ethnic Impressions

Harcourt Brace Jovanovich, Publishers

San Diego   New York   Chicago   Washington, D.C.   Atlanta

London   Sydney   Toronto

ISBN: 0-15-570748-5
Library of Congress Catalog Card Number: 83-82517
Printed in the United States of America

Cover and chapter opening illustrations by Ruben De Anda.

Credits and acknowledgments begin on p. 136, which constitutes a continuation of the copyright page.

To my father,
Henry Solomon Dinkowitz,
whose ethnic impressions
became my bedtime stories
and
To my mother,
Camilia Flatow Dinkowitz,
whose example was
one of thoroughness
in going about life's tasks

PREFACE

Ports of Entry: Ethnic Impressions offers original fiction, non-fiction, and poetry from some of our best modern writers. High-intermediate to advanced students of English as a second language can study these selections profitably. Each deals with some impression of personal life. All take into account the issue of accommodation to American society. The exercises are planned to illuminate each selection as well as to advance students' reading, writing, and speaking skills to the point of sophistication they need for college work. *Ethnic Impressions*, the first book in the *Ports of Entry* series, is appropriate for a semester of work.

The selections in *Ethnic Impressions* include biography, autobiography, memoirs, dramatic monologue, interior monologue, character sketch, and oral history. The sequence of experiences described ranges from the least acculturated to the epitome of the American Establishment. In the first chapter, William Saroyan describes a cultural environment of Armenian-Americans that is virtually self-contained. In the last chapter, William Manchester describes the life of Eleanor Roosevelt, a member of the Dutch-American Establishment, and gives the flavor of her environment. The other selections present portraits of people who achieve various degrees of adaptation to American society.

To explore the issues as they emerge, the text introduces and explains such concepts as "acculturation," "assimilation," and "culture shock." The text also presents specialized vocabulary for exposition and reading strategies as well as terms that classify vocabulary, such as connotative, denotative, explicit and implicit language, and degrees of formality. (See p. 133 for a list of these terms and where students may find them in the text.)

Difficult words in the explanatory text that accompanies the selections appear either in italics with an immediate explanation or in footnotes. Difficult words in the selections appear in boldface and are defined in marginal glosses accompanying the selections. Explanations of idioms and special items appear in footnotes. A list that explains abbreviations used in the text is provided on p. 134.

In addition, exercises that follow each selection provide vocabulary practice and pronunciation aids for difficult words and phrases. The exercises also include focus on structure, short answer quizzes, and discussion questions. Classroom activities specifically designed to "get the material off the page" include instructions for role playing and skits, round robin compositions, brainstorming, and quiz writing.

I believe international students here and

abroad will be able to identify with the literature in this multiethnic anthology because the authors relate their stories with passion and style. These readers will also understand the pain, humor, and emotions the subjects feel as they try to reconcile two cultures. In turn, these portrayals shed light on the larger society itself. *Ethnic Impressions* is a port of entry to this real store of personal striving.

I wish to express my appreciation to several editors at Harcourt Brace Jovanovich. First of all, to the late William A. Pullin, who was determined that I should write this book. I had many fruitful telephone conversations with him, but, alas, never had the chance to meet him. Next, my special thanks to Albert I. Richards, my present editor, who acted with extraordinary patience and sensitivity. To Gene Carter Lettau, house editor, and Cate Safranek, production editor, my thanks for a most professional job in putting the manuscript together. They saw the overall purpose yet gave great attention to detail.

I thank Dr. Shirley Braun of Queens College, who knew William Pullin first. As a colleague and friend she has always been most supportive of my efforts. I thank Professor Richard Haven of the English Department of the University of Massachusetts in Amherst. As a longtime friend engaged in teaching literature and language skills to native speakers of English, he brought another perspective to my thinking and suggested several authors for the collection.

I thank Professor Theresa Dalle, of Memphis State University, for her careful review of the manuscript. I wish to acknowledge Professor Fred Bosco of the Italian Department of Georgetown University for sorting out the dialectic and linguistic differences in the vocabulary for the excerpt from *Mount Allegro*. I appreciate the help of Dr. Barbara Robson of the Center of Applied Linguistics in clarifying the use of the literary present tense. And I thank Lucy Altree, library assistant at the Yenching Library at Harvard University, for drawing the ideographs for the selection from *The Woman Warrior*.

Finally, there are my children. But the deepest appreciation goes to Bob, my husband, who contributed the most and also had to weather the most.

Abelle Mason

CONTENTS

Preface   vii

1. WILLIAM SAROYAN
"The Summer of the Beautiful White Horse" from *My Name Is Aram*   1

EXERCISES   9
A. Understanding the facts   9
B. Understanding the plan   9
C. Pronunciation practice   10
D. Structure practice —Forms and word order of indirect objects with verbs of "recounting"   12
E. Understanding the words and phrases—The vocabulary of acquiring something which belongs to someone else   13
F. Understanding the ideas—Concept vocabulary   14
G. Questions for discussion   14
H. Topics for oral or written composition   15

2. JERRE MANGIONE
from *Mount Allegro: A Memoir of Italian American Life*   17

EXERCISES   24
A. Understanding the plan   24
B. Understanding the facts of Section 1   25
C. Pronunciation practice   25
D. Understanding the facts of Section 2   27
E. Structure practice—Past future tense   27
F. Understanding the ideas—Concept vocabulary   28
G. Topics for discussion   29

3. RICHARD RODRIGUEZ
from *The Hunger of Memory: The Education of Richard Rodriguez*   31

EXERCISES   36
A. Understanding the plan   36
B. Structure practice—Word order: Modifying a whole sentence with an adverb or adjective   38
C. Vocabulary practice   38
D. Understanding the ideas (for oral or written discussion)   39
E. Topics for comparison of Chapter 2, *Mount Allegro*, and Chapter 3, *Hunger of Memory*   40
F. Optional exercises   41

4. MAXINE HONG KINGSTON
from *The Woman Warrior: Memoirs of a Girlhood among Ghosts*   43

EXERCISES   47
A. Understanding the plan—Chronological or topical organization   47
B. Structure focus—Choice of tense in paragraph 1   48
C. Pronunciation practice—Phrases for rhythm, stress, and pitch   49
D. Understanding the ideas   51
E. Topics for discussion and comparison   52

5. THOMAS S. WHITECLOUD
from **"Blue Winds Dancing"**   55

EXERCISES   58
A. Understanding the
    plan—Paragraph 1: Setting the
    frame   58
B. Structure focus—Sentence
    fragments   58
C. Language focus—Repetition of
    words and phrases and use of
    parallel structure for emphasis and
    clarity   60
D. Understanding the
    plan—Development of the theme   60
E. Topics for discussion   61

6. TOSHIO MORI
    **"The Woman Who Makes Swell
    Doughnuts"** from *Yokohama,
    California*   **63**

EXERCISES   67
A. Understanding the plan—A
    characterization   67
B. Vocabulary study—Degrees of
    formality   67
C. Figures of speech—Metaphor and
    simile   68
D. Structure focus—Editing—Four
    error types   69
E. Understanding the
    ideas—Questions for discussion   72
F. Topics for writing   72

7. LANGSTON HUGHES
    "Mother to Son" from *The Weary
    Blues*
    "Harlem" from *Montage of a Dream
    Deferred*   **75**

EXERCISES for "Mother to Son"   76
A. Understanding the form—Free
    verse   76
B. More about the form—Analogy and
    dramatic monologue   77
C. Structure and rhythm   78
D. Vocabulary practice   81
E. Composition topics   81

EXERCISES for "Harlem"   82
A. Structure and form   82
B. Vocabulary—The denotation and
    connotation of words and phrases   83
C. Classifying the ideas   84
D. Topics for discussion   85

8. **"Morris Horowitz"** The life history
    of a Russian-Jewish immigrant in
    Chicago as recounted in the Federal
    Writers' Project in 1939   **87**

EXERCISES   92
A. Intensive versus extensive reading;
    Skimming and scanning   92
B. Understanding the specific events   93
C. Getting an overview of Morris
    Horowitz' life   93
D. Role playing (optional activity)   94
E. Topics for library research   94

9. EDWIN O'CONNOR
    from **"The 'Boy' Fragment"**   **97**

EXERCISES   110
A. Getting the facts of the "Boy's"
    world   110
B. Exploring the language—The use of
    irony and sarcasm in the dialogue   112
C. Vocabulary practice   114
D. Topics for discussion and writing   114

10. WILLIAM MANCHESTER
    "Eleanor, Portrait of an American"
    from *The Glory and the Dream: A
    Narrative History of America,
    1932–1972*   **117**

EXERCISES   122
A. Understanding Manchester's
    approach   122
B. Organization focus—Coherence:
    The threads that bind   122
C. Paragraph study—The effective use
    of short paragraphs   123
D. Exploring the ideas that unify the
    sketch   124
E. Topics for discussion   124
F. Topics for library research   125

Appendix of Grammar and Usage   126
For Further Reference   130
Answer Key   131
Terms of Exposition and Concept
    Vocabulary Studied   133
Abbreviations Used in the Text   134
Pronunciation Key   134
Glossary Index   137

PORTS OF ENTRY
Ethnic Impressions

1

WILLIAM SAROYAN

"The Summer of the Beautiful White Horse"

from *My Name Is Aram*

William Saroyan (1908–1981) was best known as a playwright and short story writer. His play *The Time of Your Life* won a Pulitzer Prize[1] in 1940. Between 1934 and 1940 he wrote over 500 stories. His story "The Man on the Flying Trapeze,"[*] written in 1934, won the O'Henry Short Story Award[2] of that year. *My Name Is Aram*, a collection of stories written in 1940, begins with "The Summer of the Beautiful White Horse," which we will read here.

The story is set in the countryside around Fresno, California. Saroyan was born in Fresno of Armenian immigrants and spent many of his growing up years in the area around this city. The world of Saroyan's writings is, as one critic described it, "the world of a child: vibrant,[†] powerfully simple, with everything larger than life" (Peter Sourian, *The New York Times Book Review*, 2 April, 1972).

[*]trapeze—a short bar hung from two ropes which acrobats and gymnasts use.
[†]vibrant—alive, exciting.
[1]Pulitzer Prize—a group of annual prizes in journalism, literature, and music established by Joseph Pulitzer (1847–1911), a journalist and publisher.
[2]O'Henry Short Story Award—an annual prize established for the short story writer William S. Porter (1862–1910) who wrote under the pen name of "O'Henry."

The Summer of the Beautiful White Horse

ONE day back there in the good old days when I 1
was nine and the world was full of every imaginable kind of magnificence, and life was still a
delightful and mysterious dream, my cousin Mourad,
who was considered crazy by everybody who knew him
except me, came to my house at four in the morning and
woke me up by tapping on the window of my room.

Aram, he said.

I jumped out of bed and looked out the window.   3

I couldn't believe what I saw.

It wasn't morning yet, but it was summer and with 5
daybreak not many minutes around the corner of the
world it was light enough for me to know I wasn't
dreaming.

My cousin Mourad was sitting on a beautiful white
horse.

I stuck my head out of the window and rubbed my 7
eyes.

Yes, he said in Armenian. It's a horse. You're not
dreaming. Make it quick if you want to ride.

I knew my cousin Mourad enjoyed being alive 9
more than anybody else who had ever fallen into the
world by mistake, but this was more than even I could
believe.

In the first place, my earliest memories had been
memories of horses and my first **longings** had been   **longings**   strongly felt desires
longings to ride.

This was the wonderful part.   11

In the second place, we were poor.

This was the part that wouldn't permit me to be- 13
lieve what I saw.

We were poor. We had no money. Our whole tribe
was **poverty-stricken**. Every branch of the Garoghlan-   **poverty-stricken**   extremely
ian family was living in the most amazing and comical   poor
poverty* in the world. Nobody could understand where
we ever got money enough to keep us with food in our

*comical poverty—"We were so poor it was funny."

bellies, not even the old men of the family. Most important of all, though, we were famous for our honesty. We had been famous for honesty for something like eleven centuries, even when we had been the wealthiest family in what we like to think was the world. We were proud first, honest next, and after that we believed in right and wrong. None of us would **take advantage of** anybody in the world, **let alone** steal.

Consequently, even though I could *see* the horse, so magnificent; even though I could *smell* it, so lovely; even though I could *hear* it breathing, so exciting; I couldn't *believe* the horse had anything to do with my cousin Mourad or with me or with any of the other members of our family, asleep or awake, because I *knew* my cousin Mourad couldn't have *bought* the horse, and if he couldn't have bought it he must have *stolen* it, and I refused to believe he had stolen it.

No member of the Garoghlanian family could be a **thief**.

I **stared** first at my cousin and then at the horse. There was a **pious** stillness and humor in each of them which on the one hand delighted me and on the other frightened me.

Mourad, I said, where did you steal this horse?

Leap out of the window, he said, if you want to ride.

It was true, then. He *had* stolen the horse. There was no question about it. He had come to invite me to ride or not, as I chose.

Well, it seemed to me stealing a horse for a ride was not the same thing as stealing something else, such as money. For all I knew, maybe it wasn't stealing at all. If you were crazy about horses the way my cousin Mourad and I were, it wasn't stealing. It wouldn't become stealing until we offered to sell the horse, which of course I knew we would never do.

Let me put on some clothes, I said.

All right, he said, but hurry.

I leaped into my clothes.

I jumped down to the yard from the window and leaped up onto the horse behind my cousin Mourad.

belly   *inf.*, stomach

to take advantage of   here, to try to benefit from unfairly

let alone steal   especially not to steal

thief   one who steals

to stare at   look at with eyes open and unmoving

pious   religious in manner

That year we lived at the edge of town, on Walnut Avenue. Behind our house was the country: vineyards, orchards, irrigation ditches, and country roads. In less than three minutes we were on Olive Avenue, and then the horse began **to trot**. The air was new and lovely to breathe. The feel of the horse running was wonderful. My cousin Mourad who was considered one of the craziest members of our family began to sing. I mean, he began **to roar**.

Every family has **a crazy streak** in it somewhere, 27 and my cousin Mourad was considered the natural descendant* of the crazy streak in our tribe. Before him was our uncle Khosrove, an enormous man with a powerful head of black hair and the largest mustache in the San Joaquin Valley, a man so furious in temper, so **irritable**, so impatient that he stopped anyone from talking by roaring, *It is no harm; pay no attention to it*.

That was all, no matter what anybody happened to be talking about. Once it was his own son Arak running eight blocks to the barber shop where his father was having his mustache trimmed to tell him their house was on fire. This man Khosrove sat up in the chair and roared, It is no harm, pay no attention to it. The barber said, But the boy says your house is on fire. So Khosrove roared, Enough, it is no harm, I say.

My cousin Mourad was considered the natural de- 29 scendant of this man, although Mourad's father was Zorab, who was practical and nothing else. That's how it was in our **tribe**. A man could be the father of his son's flesh, but that did not mean that he was also the father of his spirit. The distribution of the various kinds of spirit of our tribe had been from the beginning **capricious** and **vagrant**.

We rode and my cousin Mourad sang. For all anybody knew we were still in the old country where, at least according to some of our neighbors, we belonged. We let the horse run as long as it felt like running.

At last my cousin Mourad said, Get down. I want 31 to ride alone.

Will you let me ride alone? I said.

to trot   move more quickly than "to walk"

to roar   make a loud lionlike sound

a crazy streak   a line or element of craziness

irritable   easily angered

tribe   cultural, social, or racial group usually at a pre-national stage

capricious   by impulse

vagrant   moving around without a particular direction

*descendant—one of a succeeding generation in a family line. For example, a great-grandchild is a descendant of his or her great-grandparents.

That **is up to** the horse, my cousin said. Get down.   **33** to be up to   here, be the choice of

The *horse* will let me ride, I said.

We shall see, he said. Don't forget that I **have a way** **35** to have a way with   have a natural ability to handle
with a horse.

Well, I said, any way you have with a horse, I have also.

For the sake of your safety, he said, let us hope so. **37** Get down.

All right, I said, but remember you've got to let me try to ride alone.

I got down and my cousin Mourad kicked his heels **39** into the horse and shouted, *Vazire*, run. The horse stood on its **hind** legs, **snorted**, and **burst** into a fury of speed   hind   back part of
that was the loveliest thing I had even seen. My cousin   snort   noisy, nasal sound
Mourad raced the horse across a field of dry grass to an   to burst   break open by internal pressure
irrigation **ditch**, crossed the ditch on the horse, and five   ditch   a hole or channel in the ground
minutes later returned, dripping wet.

The sun was coming up.

Now it's my turn to ride, I said.   **41**

My cousin Mourad got off the horse.

Ride, he said.   **43**

I leaped to the back of the horse and for a moment knew the awfulest fear imaginable. The horse did not move.

Kick into his muscles, my cousin Mourad said. **45** What are you waiting for? We've got to take him back before everybody in the world is up and about.

I kicked into the muscles of the horse. Once again it reared and snorted. Then it began to run. I didn't know what to do. Instead of running across the field to the irrigation ditch the horse ran down the road to the vineyard of Dikran Halabian where it began to leap over vines. The horse leaped over seven vines before I fell. Then it continued running.

My cousin Mourad came running down the road. **47**

I'm not worried about you, he shouted. We've got to get that horse. You go this way and I'll go this way. If you come upon him, be kindly. I'll be near.

I continued down the road and my cousin Mourad **49** went across the field toward the irrigation ditch.

It took him half an hour to find the horse and bring him back.

All right, he said, jump on. The whole world is 51
awake now.

What will we do? I said.

Well, he said, we'll either take him back or hide him 53
until tomorrow morning.

He didn't sound worried and I knew he'd hide him
and not take him back. Not for a while, at any rate.

Where will we hide him? I said.   55

I know a place, he said.

How long ago did you steal this horse? I said.   57

It suddenly **dawned on me** that he had been taking   **it dawned on me**   it occurred to
these early morning rides for some time and had come   me
for me this morning only because he knew how much I
longed to ride.

Who said anything about stealing a horse? he said. 59

Anyhow, I said, how long ago did you begin riding
every morning?

Not until this morning, he said.   61

Are you telling the truth? I said.

Of course not, he said, but if we are **found out** 63   **to be found out**   have one's
that's what you're to say. I don't want both of us to be   secret discovered
liars. All you know is that we started riding this
morning.

All right, I said.

He walked the horse quietly to the barn of a de- 65
serted vineyard which at one time had been the pride of
a farmer named Fertajian. There were some **oats** and   **oats, alfalfa**   here, food for
dry **alfalfa** in the barn.   animals

We began walking home.

It wasn't easy, he said, to get the horse to behave so 67
nicely. At first it wanted to run wild, but, as I've told
you, I have a way with a horse. I can get it to want to do
anything *I* want it to do. Horses understand me.

How do you do it? I said.

I have an understanding with a horse, he said.   69

Yes, but what sort of an understanding? I said.

A simple and honest one, he said.   71

Well, I said, I wish I knew how to reach an understanding like that with a horse.

You're still a small boy, he said. When you get to be 73
thirteen you'll know how to do it.

I went home and ate a **hearty** breakfast.

That afternoon my uncle Khosrove came to our 75 house for coffee and cigarettes. He sat in the parlor, **sipping** and smoking and remembering the old country. Then another visitor arrived, a farmer named John Byro, an Assyrian who, out of loneliness, had learned to speak Armenian. My mother brought the lonely visitor coffee and tobacco and he rolled a cigarette and sipped and smoked, and then at last, **sighing** sadly, he said, My white horse which was stolen last month is still gone. I cannot understand it.

My uncle Khosrove became very irritated and shouted, It's no harm. What is the loss of a horse? Haven't we all lost the homeland? What is this crying over a horse?

That may be all right for you, a city dweller, to say, 77 John Byro said, but what of my **surrey**? What good is a surrey without a horse?

Pay no attention to it, my uncle Khosrove roared.

I walked ten miles to get here, John Byro said.   79

You have legs, my uncle Khosrove shouted.

My left leg pains me, the farmer said.   81

Pay no attention to it, my uncle Khosrove roared.

That horse cost me sixty dollars, the farmer said.   83

I **spit** on money, my uncle Khosrove said.

He got up and **stalked out** of the house, **slamming** 85 the screen door.

My mother explained.

He has a gentle heart, she said. It is simply that he 87 is homesick and such a large man.

The farmer went away and I ran over to my cousin Mourad's house.

He was sitting under a peach tree, trying to repair 89 the hurt wing of a young robin which could not fly. He was talking to the bird.

What is it, he said.

The farmer, John Byro, I said. He visited our house. 91 He wants his horse. You've had it a month. I want you to promise not to take it back until I learn to ride.

It will take you *a year* to learn to ride, my cousin Mourad said.

hearty large, substantial

sipping drinking slowly

to sigh take deep, audible breath

surrey light horse-drawn carriage

to spit send liquid from the mouth, often to show anger or disrespect

to stalk out walk out in anger

to slam shut with force

We could keep the horse a year, I said.   93

My cousin Mourad leaped to his feet.

What? he roared. Are you inviting a member of the 95 Garoghlanian family to steal? The horse must go back to its true owner.

When? I said.

In six months at the latest, he said.   97

He threw the bird into the air. The bird tried hard, almost fell twice, but at last flew away, high and straight.

Early every morning for two weeks my cousin 99 Mourad and I took the horse out of the barn of the deserted vineyard where we were hiding it and rode it, and every morning the horse, when it was my turn to ride alone, leaped over grape vines and small trees and threw me and ran away. Nevertheless, I hoped in time to learn to ride the way my cousin Mourad rode.

One morning on the way to Fetvajian's deserted vineyard we ran into the farmer John Byro who was on his way to town.

Let me do the talking, my cousin Mourad said. I 101 have a way with farmers.

Good morning, John Byro, my cousin Mourad said to the famer.

The farmer studied the horse eagerly.   103

Good morning, sons of my friends, he said. What is the name of your horse?

My Heart, my cousin Mourad said in Armenian.   105

A lovely name, John Byro said, for a lovely horse. I could **swear** it is the horse that was stolen from me many weeks ago. May I look into its mouth?

to swear   here, say strongly that one is speaking truthfully

Of course, Mourad said.   107

The farmer looked into the mouth of the horse.

Tooth for tooth, he said. I would swear it *is* my 109 horse if I didn't know your parents. The fame of your family for honesty is well known to me. Yet the horse is the **twin** of my horse. A suspicious man would believe his eyes instead of his heart. Good day, my young friends.

twin   one of two born of same mother at same time

Good day, John Byro, my cousin Mourad said.

Early the following morning we took the horse to 111

John Byro's vineyard and put it in the barn. The dogs followed us around without making a sound.

The dogs, I whispered to my cousin Mourad. I thought they would bark.

They would at somebody else, he said. I have a way 113 with dogs.

My cousin Mourad put his arms around the horse, pressed his nose into the horse's nose, patted it, and then we went away.

That afternoon John Byro came to our house in his 115 surrey and showed my mother the horse that had been stolen and returned.

I do not know what to think, he said. The horse is stronger than ever. **Better-tempered**, too. I thank God.

> **better-tempered** happier and more cooperative

My uncle Khosrove, who was in the parlor, be- 117 came irritated and shouted, Quiet, man, quiet. Your horse has been returned. Pay no attention to it.

EXERCISES

A. Understanding the facts

1. Who are the four main *characters* in this story, that is, the people whom the author introduces to readers? What is their relationship to each other?[3]

2. How does the *situation* or circumstances of the beautiful white horse change in the story? Who owns the horse? Who takes possession of it? Why? Where is the horse kept? Finally, about how much time passes before the horse is returned to its rightful owner?

B. Understanding the plan

1. The *narrator* of a piece is the person or character whom the author invents to tell the story. If we say that a story is told *in the first person*, we mean that the narrator uses his or her own voice, using the pronouns "I" "me" "we" "us," and so on. In such a case, the whole story is really one long quotation of the narrator's words. Often the narrator not only tells his or her views, but also participates in the events of the story.

   If the story is told *in the third person*, then the author uses the language of an observer, using the pronouns "he" "she" "they," "him" "her" "them." In that case, the writer does not participate directly in the events of the story. Furthermore, the writer may include the views of many characters as well as certain overall views.

   With this information in mind, please answer the following questions:

[3]Notice that we use the present tense to discuss literature. See Appendix.

    a. From whose point of view is the story told?

    b. Is the narration in the first person or in the third person? Give a sample sentence from the story to support your answer.

2. The events in this story are presented in *chronological order*—that is, they are presented in the same time sequence in which they occurred. These events are listed below. Number them in *chronological order*.

    _____ **a.** John Byro visits Aram's family with the beautiful white horse and remarks about its excellent condition.

    _____ **b.** Uncle Khosrove and John Byro have coffee at Aram's family's house. John Byro complains about the loss of his horse. Uncle Khosrove gets angry, slams the door, and leaves.

    _____ **c.** At 4 o'clock one morning, Mourad appears at Aram's bedroom window on horseback.

    _____ **d.** The first time that Aram mounts the horse, the horse runs away wild. Aram falls off. It takes a half hour to recover the horse.

    _____ **e.** The horse is returned to John Byro's barn.

    _____ **f.** One morning on the way back to Fetvajian's barn, Mourad and Aram, the horse with them, meet John Byro.

    _____ **g.** Aram asks Mourad not to return the horse until he, Aram, has learned to ride it.

3. To help the reader understand the sequence of events and the feelings of the characters, the author fills in some background information. Discuss when and why he provides the following information.

    a. When does the author discuss the poor but honest reputation of the Garoghlanian family? Why is this important for the reader to know?

    b. When does Saroyan discuss the crazy streak in the family? Which characters exemplify this streak? Why do you think the author brings up this information?

    c. When does Saroyan relate the incident about Uncle Khosrove in the barber shop? What happened there? Why does the author mention it?

    d. When does Saroyan mention the ethnic background of John Byro? Why does he bring this up?

C. Pronunciation practice

    Repeat the exercises after your instructor. (Note: slashes // enclose phonetic transcription of sounds.)

1. The Armenian names (with American English pronunciation):

Mourad /ˈmü-rȧd/	Garoghlanian family /ˌgar-ȧg-ˈlan-ē-ən/
Aram /ˈa-rim/	John Byro /ˈbī-rō/
Khosrove /ˈkȧz-rōv/	

Fill in the blanks and practice saying the names aloud.

a. The cousins were called _____ and _____ .

b. Uncle _____ and _____ had in common a crazy streak.

c. _____ is an Armenian family name.

2. Silent letters: muscles, clothes

"Muscles" has the same pronunciation as "mussels" /ˈməs-əlz/.

"Clothes" has the same pronunciation as the verb "close" /klōz/.

Practice saying these sentences:
a. Mussels are shellfish with strong muscles.
b. Close the clothes closet, please.

3. Reduced vowel sounds: vineyard, orchard
"Vine" and "yard" as separate words are pronounced /vīn/ and /yärd/, so that

vine rhymes with mine

yard rhymes with guard

However, when "vine" and "yard" are joined to form the compound "vineyard" /ˈvin-yərd/,

vine rhymes with in

yard rhymes with bird

In the word "orchard" /ˈor-chərd/, there is "or" + "chard" which rhymes with "bird."

Practice saying these sentences:
a. There are vines in the yards of Martha's Vineyard.[4]
b. There are birds in the orchards of Orchard Beach.[5]

4. Diphthonged u:

fury /ˈfyur-ē/   furious /ˈfyur-ē-əs/

fur /ˈfer/   furry /ˈfer-ē/

Practice saying these sentences:
a. The curious animal was furious.
b. The fury of the furry animal was curious.

5. Stress on the second syllable:

capricious /ka-ˈprish-əs, — ˈprē-shəs/[6]   facetious* /fə-ˈsē-shəs/

suspicious /sə-ˈspish-əs/   fictitious† /fik-ˈtish-əs/

Practice saying these sentences:
a. Don't be capricious or facetious.
b. Don't be suspicious. The story is fictitious.

*facetious—joking, unserious.
†fictitious—untrue, invented.
[4]Martha's Vineyard is an island belonging to Massachusetts.
[5]Orchard Beach is located in New York City.
[6]Note that "capricious" may be pronounced two ways. It can rhyme with facetious or with suspicious.

D. Structure practice—Forms and word order of indirect objects with verbs of "recounting"

1. The most common verbs of recounting are "to tell," "to explain," "to say." There are certain variations in form and word order of indirect objects which must be learned for these and several other verbs.

Let us look first at the usual word order for regular verbs such as "to send" which take direct and indirect objects:

	S	V	I.O.	D.O.	I.O.
	John	sent		a message.	
OR	John	sent		a message	<u>to</u> Mary.
	John	sent	Mary	a message.	

In this regular form, when the indirect object comes <u>after</u> the direct object, the word "to" or "for" is included. (Such a phrase—"to" or "for" plus the noun or pronoun — functions as an indirect object.) When the indirect object comes <u>before</u> the direct object, the word "to" or "for" is omitted.

The verb "to tell" follows the same form as "to send." Thus,

S	V	I.O.	D.O.	I.O.
John	told	Mary	a story.	
John	told		a story	<u>to</u> Mary.

The verbs "to say" and "to explain" operate with a certain variation:

S	V	D.O.	I.O.
John	{ said { explained	something	
John	{ said { explained	something	<u>to</u> Mary.

With these verbs the indirect object is <u>always</u> used with "to" and usually comes <u>after</u> the direct object. If the indirect object comes <u>before</u> the direct object, the "to" is still retained. Such word order is desirable when the direct object is a long phrase or a direct quotation. For example,

S	V	I.O.	D.O.
John	{ said { explained	to his friend	that he wouldn't be able to go there.
John	{ said { explained	to his friend,	"I won't be able to go there."

(The Appendix includes information on the punctuation of direct quotations.) Other verbs which operate in the same way as "to say" and "to explain" include "to relate," "to recount," "to shout," "to whisper."

2. Substitute the verb indicated. (See Appendix for notes on the verb "to tell.")

Example: He said something awful to me.
(to tell) **He told me something awful.**

(to tell)
    a. He explained the problem to me.
_____.

(to recount)
    b. He told me the story of his life.
_____.

(to whisper)
    c. He told me the secret.
_____.

(to explain)
    d. He shouted something to me which I could not understand.
_____.

3. Pick a partner and take turns recounting an incident in the story to the other person. Be sure you and your partner are using the indirect object form correctly. Be prepared to tell the incident to the class.

E. Understanding the words and phrases—The vocabulary of acquiring something which belongs to someone else

1. Acquiring something which belongs to someone else can happen in various ways: by gift, by purchase or exchange, by loan, or by theft. This story is concerned primarily with the last two: borrowing and stealing. Here is some vocabulary to express these methods:

The Activity	Verb	The Agent[7]	The Act Itself	Adjective
borrowing	to borrow	borrower	borrowing	borrowed borrowing
lending	to lend loan	lender	loan	lent loan lending
stealing	to steal	thief	theft	stolen stealing
robbing	to rob	robber (crook)	robbery	robbed robbing

2. a. Read the dialogue which takes places between two roommates, Linda and Dorothy.

LINDA: I forgot to go to the bank, and I'm very low on cash. Would you have an extra $5.00?

DOROTHY: Sure. Take it, and return it when you can.

LINDA: Thanks a lot. I'll give it back Thursday.

DOROTHY: Okay, but don't worry about it.

[7]In English, the person or party who gives the item is the _lender_; the person or party who receives the item is the _borrower_. For example, a library <u>lends</u> books; a person can <u>borrow</u> books from a library.

b. Describe the situation in the dialogue by answering the following sentences. Use the vocabulary in the "lending" section.
  i. What did Linda wish to do?
  ii. What did Dorothy do for Linda?
  iii. What did the sum of five dollars represent?
  iv. What will happen on Thursday?
c. Suppose Dorothy hadn't been home at the time and Linda took five dollars from her roommate's wallet. Would this be borrowing? Explain your answer.

F. Understanding the ideas—Concept vocabulary

Verb	*Noun*
to reason	rationale
to rationalize[8]	rationalization

When you *reason*, you follow logical steps which, one hopes, will lead to a conclusion, a judgment, or a plan. A *rationale* is the explanation for such a conclusion, judgment, or plan. Thus, a rationale is a product of reasoning.

On the other hand, when you *rationalize*, you try to find good reasons to support a decision which has already been made; that is, you try to justify what you have done. Thus a *rationalization* is a justification for a plan or decision previously set.

For example, suppose that a certain student decides to go to the movies rather than to study, even though he or she has a lot of homework to do. The student might think
a. I am tired of studying.
b. I deserve a change and some relaxation.
c. The movie is supposed to be excellent.
d. It will only be playing tonight.
e. I'll study much better tomorrow.
f. My professor won't mind if I hand the work in late.
  This student has been *rationalizing*. The six points are the rationalizations.

Are any of the characters in Saroyan's story rationalizing? Keep this overall question in mind as you answer 1 and 2 under Questions for Discussion.

G. Questions for discussion

1. Has the horse been stolen? Does John Byro think so? Does Mourad think so? What does Aram think? How do you define theft?

2. What is the basic conflict in Aram about the situation with the horse? That is, what are the two strong but opposite views that Aram holds regarding his conduct?

3. What do you think Saroyan's view of the matter is? What do you think his view of childhood is?

4. Uncle Khosrove has a favorite statement that he makes no matter how serious the situation is. What is this statement? Why does he ignore many practical events with this statement? (Study p. 4 particularly.)

---

[8]In math, this verb indicates a certain process. That meaning is not included here.

5. What steps does John Byro take to recover his horse? Why doesn't he tell the family or accuse the children directly about the taking of his horse? Is it important that John Byro is Assyrian? Would you say that John Byro handles his situation well? Explain your answer.

6. A number of words and expressions follow. Alone or with a partner, note those which best describe each of the characters. One item may apply to more than one character or to none. Be prepared to support your selection with examples from the story. Can you add other words or expressions to describe any of the characters? If so, fill them in.

Aram	Mourad	Descriptive Words	Uncle Khosrove	John Byro
___	___	homesick	___	___
___	___	honest	___	___
___	___	long-suffering	___	___
___	___	poor	___	___
___	___	disillusioned	___	___
___	___	placid	___	___
___	___	lazy	___	___
___	___	feeling guilty	___	___
___	___	kind	___	___
___	___	often furious	___	___
___	___	respectful	___	___
___	___	unreasonable	___	___
___	___	unsympathetic	___	___
___	___	with a crazy streak	___	___
___	___	caring about animals	___	___
___	___	fun-loving	___	___

H. Topics for oral or written compositions

1. Aram tells the story from his point of view so that we are able to sympathize with him. If Mourad or John Byro had told the story or if it had been told in the third person, we might have reacted differently to the events.
   a. Imagine that you are Mourad or John Byro thinking about the events of the story. Choose one event and write it from either of their points of view.
   b. Or, retell the important events in the third person as you would in a story.

2. As a child, were you ever in a situation such as Aram was in? Did you ever feel torn between a desire for something and your conscience telling you it was wrong? What happened and how did you resolve it? Write a paragraph in the first person recounting the experience.

2

JERRE MANGIONE

from *Mount Allegro: A Memoir of Italian American Life*

Jerre Mangione (b. 1909) is Professor Emeritus of English at the University of Pennsylvania. The body of his writing has concerned the ethnic experience of the children of immigrants to the United States. His most recent book (1978) was entitled *An Ethnic at Large—A Memoir of America in the Thirties and Forties*.

The book represented here, *Mount Allegro*, was first published by Houghton Mifflin in 1942. It deals with childhood and growing up in a Sicilian neighborhood of Rochester, New York. However, Sicily is mountainous, but Rochester is not. Professor Mangione explains the choice of title as follows:

> The name of 'Mount Allegro,' which I gave to the neighborhood where my relatives lived, occurred to me after Houghton Mifflin announced that the book would be published as fiction. The area is as flat as Kansas but since I liked the sound, I decided to use it anyway. About 20 years ago, Mount Allegro became the area's official name and is so noted in the histories of Rochester. (Edwin McDonald, "Publishing: Ethnic Classic Keeps Coming Back," *The New York Times*, 4 Sept., 1981)

Mount Allegro has been reprinted several times and has been variously classified as *fiction* and *non-fiction*. A piece of fiction is writing in which the characters, situations, and events are imaginary. A piece of non-fiction is writing other than fiction, poetry, or drama. While reading and studying the selection, try to decide whether you would classify *Mount Allegro* as fiction or non-fiction.

from **Mount Allegro**
When I Grow Up . . .

'When I grow up I want to be an American,' 1 Giustina said. We looked at our sister; it was something none of us had ever said.

'Me too,' Maria echoed.

'Aw, you don't even know what an American is,' 3 Joe **scoffed**.

to scoff   speak disrespectfully

'I do so,' Giustina said.

It was more than the rest of us knew.   5

'We're Americans right now,' I said. 'Miss Zimmerman says if you're born here you're an American.'

'Aw, **she's nuts**,' Joe said. He had no use for most 7 teachers. 'We're Italians. If y' don't believe me ask Pop.'

to be nuts   *sl.*, be crazy

But my father wasn't very helpful. 'Your children will be *Americani*. But you, my son, are half-and-half. Now stop asking me questions. You should know those things from going to school. What do you learn in school, anyway?'

The world, my teacher insisted, was made up of all 9 the colored spots on a globe. One of the purple spots was America, even though America wasn't purple when you looked at it. The orange spot was Italy. Never having been there, that wasn't so hard to believe. You never used this globe as a ball, even after Rosario Alfano gave you one as a birthday present. You just **spun** it, while some near-by grownup told you that Columbus discovered the world to be round.

spun   *p.t.* of "to spin," turn fast in circles

You pretended to believe that because it was hard to argue with grownups and be polite at the same time, but you told yourself that any grownup who **swallowed** that must be nuts. It was confusing when your own father said it because you liked to think he was right about everything; but when your Uncle Sarafino said it, the uncle from Boston who promised to give you a dollar for eating some hot peppers raw, and then refused to give you the money, you were sure he was nuts and the world wasn't round.

to swallow that   here, believe

Then one day one of your new teachers looked at 11
you brightly and said you were Italian because your last
name was Amoroso and that too was puzzling. You
talked it over with some of the boys in the gang.

First with Tony Long, who was the leader. Tony
said his father changed his name when he came to
America because he got tired of spelling it out for a lot of
dopes who didn't know how to spell. I showed Tony my
globe and he pointed to a red spot on it and said that
was where his mother and father came from. That's all
he knew about it. Tony couldn't speak Polish and his
mother hardly knew any American. He looked angry when she spoke to him in Polish in front of the
other kids.

> **dope** *sl.*, a stupid person

Then there was Abe Rappaport, who went to a 13
synagogue every Saturday. Abe wore glasses and knew
a lot. He said his parents came from Russia and pointed
to a big **gob** of blue on the globe. It was close to Poland
but Abe looked more like me than he did like Tony, who
had blond hair. . . .

> **gob** *sl.*, a large mass

I showed my globe to a guy who belonged to another gang. His name was Robert Di Nella and he had
blond hair and blue eyes like Tony Long. . . . He
pointed to Italy on the globe, even though his mother
didn't speak Italian the way mine did. Then he pointed
to a tiny orange splash at the end of the Italian boot and
called me a lousy *Siciliano*. I hit him on the jaw, and
because he was taller and bigger, ran to safety with the
globe **tucked** under my arm like a football.

> *Siciliano* *Ital.*, a Sicilian, person from Sicily
>
> **to tuck** fold or place in a small, safe place

This incident marked the beginning of a long and 15
violent feud. . . . He **ambushed** me at every possible
opportunity and preceded each attack by calling me a
Sicilian. . . .

> **to ambush** lie in wait and then attack

Family Party

Before they became Americanized enough to learn
poker, my father and three of my uncles used to play
briscola on Sunday afternoons. It was a fine game to

> **poker** a card game
>
> *briscola* *Ital.*, a card game

watch because it was played with partners, and the rules permit the partners to signal each other throughout the playing. . . .

The same partners always played together and were so familiar with their signal systems that they could talk about the European War or the high price of food without ever **losing track** of the game. . . .

to lose track of   fail to follow

The women sat near the card table, sewing and **gossiping** about the women who were not present, . . .

to gossip   talk about details of other people's lives

We children made the most noise, each one trying to surpass the other with **earsplitting shrieks**. Our only concern was **to steer clear of** adults who might become irritated enough **to cuff** us. . . .

earsplitting   here, extremely loud

shriek   a loud cry

to steer clear of   keep out of the way of

to cuff   slap or hit lightly

Toward sunset, when the wives got hungry and tired of gossiping, they would **give due notice** that it was time to set the table. Since the same table was used for eating and playing cards, it was a polite way of telling the men to stop their game. After a great deal of skillful **procrastination**, the men would play their 'last' game and **settle their accounts**. This was a distinctive moment in our lives because one of the winners would be sure to give us pennies, or someone would drop a coin on the floor. Whenever that happened, one of the men would always say, 'Let the servants have it.' This was a standing joke among my relatives which they had inherited from their fathers and grandfathers, who, like themselves, had never had enough money to afford servants.

to give due notice   say properly in advance

procrastination   putting off of something which should be done

to settle their accounts   pay money owed and receive money due

The losers would **dispatch** one of us to the neighboring saloon for a bucket of beer, and the women would spread a white tablecloth over the table and pile it high with fried Italian sausages, *pizza* made with cheese and tomatoes, and fried artichokes if they were in season. Finally there would come a great silence, the silence of hungry people eating tasty food, broken only by the children, whose interest in food was still undeveloped. At such occasions we could hold the center of the stage, for then and only then was it possible **to risk** the **impropriety** of speaking at the table while food was being eaten.

to dispatch   send

to risk   take a chance

impropriety   socially unsuitable act

Ordinarily, of course, a meal was more than a meal; it was a **ritual** and only adults were allowed to carry on

ritual   custom or ceremony

any conversation. They were the high priests, and if a child dared open his mouth without first being addressed by one of them, it would surely cost him a scolding* and possibly a meal. But on Sunday nights speaking during meals was a special dispensation†— and we made the most of it. Many of our questions would go unanswered, but we asked them anyway, just for the joy of talking at meals without **being reprimanded**.

to reprimand   scold in a formal way

It was futile to expect any intelligent responses 23 until the fruit and coffee were served. Then the men would take out their pipes and cigarettes and **deign** to talk at us. They talked in adult language, without any regard for our ages. . . .

to deign   lower oneself or condescend to do

One Sunday night stands out clearly. . . . I felt an urgent need to know more about Sicily if I was going to continue taking beatings for it. I wanted to know what the difference was between Sicily and Italy, and whether Sicily was a nation or a city. . . .

'*Santa Maria!* You mean to tell me you don't know 25 what Sicily is?' My Uncle Luigi was shocked by my question.

'What do they teach you in school, anyway? At your age—how old are you, anyway? Nine? Why, when I was nine I knew all about the United States. Can *you* name the forty-six states in the Union alphabetically?'

'There are forty-eight states,‡ *Ziu.*'

27 *Ziu*   Sicil., uncle

'There were forty-six when I learned them, and I learned them right. Don't contradict me. Don't they teach you the meaning of respect in school? . . . Well,' he **rambled**, reaching for his **snuff**, 'Sicily was never as large as the United States but once it was the world's garden of culture.'

to ramble   talk or walk in aimless way

snuff   tobacco made into powder for breathing in

'Don't fill the child's head with a lot of nonsense 29 about culture,' said my redheaded Uncle Nino, who was more cultured than any of my relatives. 'Sicily is

---

*it would surely cost him a scolding—an adult would get angry with him for doing something wrong.

†special dispensation—permission to break the general rule. The Catholic Church sometimes gives this kind of special permission.

‡It was not until 1959 when Alaska and Hawaii became states that there were 50 states in the nation.

beautiful, yes. So beautiful, in fact, that I should like nothing better than to return there. But it is also terribly poor. It lies at the end of the Italian boot and some government **clique** in Rome is always **kicking it around**. Some Sicilians got tired of that treatment and finally left. That, Gerlando, is the chief reason most of us are in this *maliditta terra*, where we spend our strength in factories and ditches and think of nothing but money. All that journeying and all that work just so that we might live and die with our bellies full.' He dug his fork into another piece of sausage by way of punctuation. As a matter of fact, he had never worked in either a factory or a ditch or done a stroke of hard work,* but we were all too polite to point that out to him.

'Your Uncle Nino is right about Sicily's poverty,' my father said. 'Sicily is not far from Rome, only a day or two by slow train, but few Sicilians every had the money to go there.' He looked sad.

'Some day, my son, you will go and see Sicily for 31 yourself,' my father said. 'You will see many lovely women and golden sunsets on a blue sea. You will see olive trees that look as old as the world itself. My father, *bonarma*, once told me that God must have once decided to make Sicily the Garden of Eden and then changed his mind abruptly. You will see what he meant when you go. But you must also expect to see *la miseria*. It is all around like a sickness.'

'You are filling the child's head with a lot of crazy ideas. Sicily is one of the most beautiful lands in the world.' My mother was **vehement**. No one dared answer her. 'Sicily,' she continued **defiantly**, 'has fruits and flowers beyond the imagination of Americans and, besides, it is the place where your father and mother were born. Most of us did not have much schooling, but we have as much culture and courtesy as Italians who weren't born in Sicily. Don't forget that.'

My mother could always be depended on for her 33 common sense.

'You won't forget, will you?' she repeated.

clique   a small, closely united group who do not let others join easily

to kick around   here, treat badly

maliditta terra   *Sicil.*, cursed land

bonarma   *Sicil.*, blessed soul

la miseria   *Sicil.*, misery and suffering

vehement   expressing strong emotion

defiantly   fearlessly refusing to obey or agree

*to do a stroke of hard work—usually used negatively to describe a lazy person.

'No, I won't,' I promised, **lapsing** into English.

'Don't speak American to me,' she **snapped**. 'I don't want to hear anything but Italian in this house. You will never learn it anywhere else. I don't want *my* children to grow up into *babbi* who can't speak the language of their parents.'

There were seldom less than fifteen men, women, and children at those Sunday sessions; on the Sundays when it rained, there would be as many as thirty. It was obvious that no one else in Mount Allegro had as many relatives as I did; it was also true that no one else's relatives seemed to seek one another's company as much as mine did. Sundays or weekdays, they were as **gregarious** as ants but had a far more pleasant time. There were always relatives and friends present or about to arrive. And when they finally left for the night, they occasionally came back for a surprise visit which they called a *sirinata*.

On these occasions they brought food, as well as their mandolins and guitars. They stood under our bedroom windows and sang gently until some member of the household awoke; and when they saw a light go on their singing became louder and more joyous, breaking into an **uproarious crescendo** as the door was opened to them. The only neighbors who ever **minded** were those who were not Sicilians. The others would call out greetings from their bedroom windows, obviously hoping that they would be invited.

The explanations for the serenades were invariably the same: 'There were so many stars out tonight that it seemed a pity to go to bed,' or, 'So-and-so couldn't get to sleep and thought you might enjoy a little music.' It was unnecessary apologizing because everyone was very happy to see each other again, after an **interim** of almost two hours, but my relatives could always be counted on to observe the amenities,* especially when they seemed most unnecessary.

Since there were never any rules against children's staying up as long as they wished, we joined these

35 to lapse into   slip into unintentionally

to snap   make a sudden, sharp sound

babbi   Sicil., idiots

37

gregarious   liking society, being "as social as ants"

sirinata   Sicil., serenade

uproarious crescendo   with increasing noise and laughter

to mind   here, oppose, be against

39

interim   the time in between

*to observe the amenities—follow polite and considerate behavior and social forms.

revelries. It was impossible to sleep anyway. The joking and the singing of our elders were **too much to resist**, and we sat on the edges of the room in our nightshirts watching them **solemnly**, a little **shocked** to discover that they could be as noisy and carefree as we could. Those with good voices sang **mournful** solos about love and death; the relatives with ordinary voices sang **bawdy ditties** that made the women **giggle** and the children blush, even though we understood only an occasional *double-entendre*.

The party was punctuated by my father's trips to the wine cellar, and his emergence with more wine and a new set of amazing **puns**. Every half-hour or so one of the women would dutifully remark that it was getting late, whereupon my father would **shush her** with the proposal for another drink and another song. Finally, even he became tired and the company would start saying good-bye. These farewells were as **lingering** as the death scene in an opera, and **were couched in** such terms of endearment* that no one could possibly suspect that these same persons would be seeing each other again in a couple of days, if not sooner.

41

revelry   noisy dancing, eating, and drinking

too much to resist   too tempting or inviting

solemnly   in a serious manner

shocked   here, uncomfortably surprised

mournful   sad

bawdy ditties   funny songs in verse about sex

to giggle   laugh, usually in a high voice

double-entendre   having two meanings, one of which often refers to sex

pun   an amusing use of a word or phrase which has two meanings

to shush her   keep her quiet

lingering   slow to end

to be couched in   be phrased in

*terms of endearment—special words of love, such as "dear" or "darling" in English.

EXERCISES

A. Understanding the plan

1. A *biography* is a piece of writing in which the author gives an account of another person's life. An *autobiography* is a piece of writing in which the author gives an account of his or her own life. A *memoir*—or memoirs—is a kind of writing which emphasizes memories and impressions of a person's life, either one's own or someone else's. Therefore, a memoir may be less complete or give fewer facts than a biography or autobiography would.

   The book *Mount Allegro* has been described as something between an autobiography and a memoir. Would you expect, therefore, to find the writing in the first person or in the third person? Look at the selection and find a sample sentence which shows in which person the selection is actually written.

2. If *Mount Allegro* were a true autobiography, you would expect the narrator's name to be the same as the author's name; that is, Jerre Mangione. In this case, however, the author

tells the story from the point of view of Gerlando Amoroso. Mangione also changes the names of the other members of his family. He does this, he says, in order to give the book a fictional quality.

3. An *excerpt* is a piece taken from a book, speech, or musical work. The selection here is made up of several short excerpts from the first two chapters of Mangione's book. These chapters give the flavor of his childhood.

B. Understanding the facts of Section 1

1. The Situation: Section 1, "When I Grow Up . . . ," begins with a conversation. Who takes part in the discussion? How old do you think they are? What is the subject of the conversation?

2. National Identity: The national identity of the narrator is described in five different ways.
   a. Which character describes the narrator in these various ways? Fill in the name of the person or persons next to what they said. (Then check the Answer Key.)
      (1) You are American. _____
      (2) You are Italian. _____
      (3) You are Sicilian. _____
      (4) You are half American and half Italian; your children will be American. _____
      (5) You may grow up to be American. _____
   b. What is the legal status of the narrator's nationality? How do you explain the other interpretations?
   c. What is a generation and how long is it? What does *first generation* mean? What does *second generation* mean? Give an example of someone in the reading or a well-known person who is first generation American. Give an example of someone who is second generation American.
   d. The narrator mentions students of various national origins. Identify these other national origins.

C. Pronunciation practice

Repeat the exercises after your instructor. (Slashes // enclose phonetic transcription sounds.)

1. The Italian names (with American English pronunciation):

   Gerlando Amoroso /ger-ˈlan-dō/ /ˌȧ-mō-ˈrō-sō/

   Uncle Sarafino /ˌsȧ-rȧ-ˈfē-nō/

   Uncle Luigi /Lü-ˈē-gē/

   Uncle Nino /ˈnī-nō/

   a. The narrator's name was _____ _____ .
   b. The father used to play cards with three uncles: Uncle _____; Uncle _____ ; and Uncle _____ .

2. Italian words (with American English pronunciation):

briscola /bris-ˈcō-là/

sirinata /ˌsir-i-ˈnä-tà/

a. On Sunday afternoon the men in the family played _____ .
b. On Sunday evening the relatives often returned for a _____ .

3. Stress on the first syllable:

vehement /ˈvē-ə-mənt/ ·

interim /ˈin-tə-rəm, -rim/

ritual /ˌrich-(ə-)wəl, ˈrich-əl/

revelry /ˈrev-əl-rē/

reprimand /ˈrep-rə-ˌmand/

Practice saying these sentences:
a. There was an interim of vehement revelry.
b. This was followed by a ritual of reprimand.

4. The /ä/ sound:
When a doctor wishes to look in your throat he may say, "Open your mouth and say 'Ah' /ä/." This vowel sound occurs in the following words:

blond
gob
gossip
synagogue /ˈsin-i-ˌgäg/

Practice saying these sentences:
a. There was a blue gob in the picture of the synagogue.
b. It represented the blond gossip.

5. The *vowel sounds* in the following words from the selection are the same as the familiar words on the left:

Pain /pān/ rhymes with deign /dān/   /ā/
Fun /fən/ rhymes with sun /sən/   /ə/
Peak /pēk/ rhymes with clique /klēk/   /ē/

6. Practice the rhythm of the underlined words by saying

Gregarious /gri-ˈgar-ē-əs, -ˈger-/, hilarious /hil-ˈar-ē-əs, -hil-ˈer-/: the people are quite various /ˈvar-ē-əs, -ˈver-/.

D. Understanding the facts of Section 2

1. The Situation: Section 2, "Family Party," occurs on a Sunday beginning in the afternoon. Where does the gathering take place? What are the men doing? What are the women doing? What about the children?

2. Movement toward the second event begins around sunset. What is that event? What are the steps of preparation and change?

3. In what ways is the Sunday evening meal different from other meals throughout the week?

4. The final event of the evening is a *sirinata*. How many people may participate? What customarily occurs?

   Consider the events of a typical Sunday in *Mount Allegro* in terms of the following adjectives.

noisy	lighthearted	friendly
quiet	hilarious	inviting
serious	uproarious /ˌə-ˈprōr-ē-əs, -ˈpròr-/	sentimental
gregarious	familial	carefree
formal	ritualistic /ˌrich-(ə-)wal-ˈis-tik, ˌrich-əl-/	warmhearted

   What adjectives would you apply to the activities at the evening meal of
   the men? _____
   the women? _____
   the children? _____
   What adjectives would you apply to the activities at the evening meal of
   the adults? _____
   the children? _____
   What adjectives would you apply to the atmosphere of the *sirinata*? _____

E. Structure practice—Past future tense

1. One use of the past future tense is to recount events that were typical, customary, or likely to occur during a period of time in the past. It is formed by using <u>would</u> + <u>base form of verb</u>: "would do."

2. Study the following examples to see how the past future tense contrasts with the simple past and habitual past tenses:

   Simple Past: On Sunday, the men <u>played</u> cards around the dining room table.
   The meaning here is either of a single event, such as referring to last Sunday, or a recurring event, such as on Sunday of every week, the men played cards. To understand the exact meaning we would need additional information.

   Habitual Past: On Sunday, the men <u>used to play</u> cards.
   The meaning here is that on Sunday of every week the men played cards.

Past Future: On Sunday, the men <u>would play</u> cards.

The meaning here is that on most Sundays it was likely that the men played cards; on a typical Sunday, they did so. (See Appendix for other uses of the past future tense.)

3. Here is an example of the past future tense found in the reading:

"After a great deal of procrastination, the men <u>would play</u> their 'last' game and settle their accounts."

Write down two other sentences from the reading which use this tense.

4. Think of an event or holiday which you experienced or participated in a number of times. Recount the sequence of events which were likely to take place. Use the past future tense wherever appropriate. However, do not force the language or ideas. If necessary, use other tenses, too.

F. Understanding the ideas—Concept vocabulary

Acculturation

When one group of people comes to live in the culture of another, the members of that group must make certain *adaptations* or changes in their habits in order to manage in a comfortable way. There is the common expression which goes, "When in Rome do as the Romans do." That is, you adopt some of the habits and style of behavior that the people in the host country or setting do. For example, you shake hands or bow in greeting as people in that culture do. *Acculturation* is this process of adopting the social patterns of another group.

Assimilation

A step beyond acculturation involves *assimilation* or the adopting of cultural traits. The expression quoted above might be changed to "Come to Rome; become a Roman." In that case, assimilation would mean to "become a Roman" in a cultural, non-biological sense.

Sense of Identity

"Who am I?" We know who we are in terms of our background, our family, our neighborhood, our cultural and national communities, and so on. This knowledge gives us our *sense of identity*. Social and cultural adaptation carries with it changes in one's sense of identity. In other words, our sense of identity or the answer to "Who am I?" becomes more complex as one adapts to a new culture.

The people—both children and grownups—in *Mount Allegro* were trying *to come to terms with* their changing national and cultural identity; that is, they were trying to understand their evolving* situation and how it related to their cultural roots.

Exercise

1. When Giustina says, in the first sentence of Section 1, "When I grow up I want to be an American," is she talking about acculturation or assimilation? Explain your answer.

*evolving—changing and growing.

2. When the narrator says, in the first sentence of Section 2, "Before they became Americanized enough to learn poker, my father and three uncles used to play *briscola* on Sunday afternoons," is he talking about acculturation or assimilation? Explain your answer.

G. Topics for discussion

1. Discuss the attitudes of the characters that would lead to acculturation and assimilation and those that would retain the customs of Sicily. Consider the attitudes toward the family as a group; toward speaking Italian and English; toward Sicily as a community as compared to the United States.

2. Compare Uncle Khosrove in "The Summer of the Beautiful White Horse" and Gerlando's father in *Mount Allegro*. How do their personalities differ? How much is their sense of identity rooted in the country where they were born, and how much in the United States? Give examples to support your views.

3

RICHARD RODRIGUEZ

from *The Hunger of Memory: The Education of Richard Rodriguez*

Richard Rodriguez (b. 1944) is of a later generation than Mangione. He writes about going to elementary school in the 1950s, while Mangione's memories of childhood go back 30 to 35 years before. Interestingly, both men wanted to be professors of English literature and writers. Both had the opportunity to pursue these careers although their life patterns were quite different.

In an article which appeared in 1974, Rodriguez said,

> I am the son of Mexican-American parents, who speak a blend
> of Spanish and English, but who read neither language easily. I
> am about to receive a Ph.D. in English Renaissance[1] literature.
> What sort of life—what tensions, feelings, conflicts—connects
> these two sentences?

The selection we will read here from the book *The Hunger of Memory* (1981) deals with some of the differences Rodriguez found between home and school in his early years.

Rodriguez was born in California. He attended parochial schools* in Sacramento, and did his undergraduate work at Stanford University. He went on to study at Columbia University, at the Warburg Institute in London as a Fulbright Scholar, and finally at the University of California, Berkeley, where he received the Ph.D. degree. He lives today as a writer in San Francisco.

---

*parochial schools—church schools.

[1]The Renaissance was a period beginning about A.D. 1500 which marked a rebirth of interest in classical studies.

from The Hunger of Memory

[I] I remember, to start with, that day in Sacramento— 1 a California now nearly thirty years past—when I first entered a classroom, able to understand some fifty **stray** English words.

stray scattered, unconnected

The third of four children, I had been preceded to a neighborhood Roman Catholic school by an older brother and sister. But neither of them had revealed very much about their classroom experiences. Each afternoon they returned, as they left in the morning, always together, speaking in Spanish as they climbed the five steps of the porch. And their mysterious books, wrapped in shopping-bag paper, remained on the table next to the door, closed firmly behind them.

An accident of geography sent me to a school 3 where all my classmates were white, many the children of doctors and lawyers and business executives. All my classmates certainly must have been uneasy on that first day of school—as most children are uneasy—to find themselves apart from their families in the first institution of their lives. But I was astonished.

The nun* said, in a friendly but oddly impersonal voice, 'Boys and girls, this is Richard Rodriguez.' (I heard her sound out: *Rich-heard Road-ree-guess*.) It was the first time I had heard anyone name me in English. 'Richard,' the nun repeated more slowly, writing my name down in her black leather book. Quickly I turned to see my mother's face dissolve in a watery **blur** behind the pebbled glass door. . . .

blur unclear, indistinct effect

[II] In the early years of my boyhood, my parents 5 **coped** very well in America. My father had steady work. My mother managed at home. They were nobody's victims. Optimism and ambition led them to a house (our home) many blocks from the Mexican south side of town. We lived among *gringos* and only a block from

coped managed

los gringos Sp., here, English-speaking North Americans

*nun—a woman who has joined a religious group, such as an order of the Catholic Church, to live a life of prayer, service, and obedience. Nuns can be nurses or teachers or have other professions.

the biggest, whitest houses. It never occurred to my parents that they couldn't live wherever they chose. Nor was the Sacramento of the fifties **bent on** teaching them a contrary lesson. My mother and father were more annoyed than **intimidated** by those two or three neighbors who tried initially to make us unwelcome. ('Keep your **brats** away from my sidewalk!') But despite all they achieved, perhaps because they had so much to achieve, any deep feeling of ease, the confidence of 'belonging' in public was withheld from them both. They regarded the people at work, the faces in crowds, as very distant from us. They were the others, *los gringos*. That term was interchangeable in their speech with another, even more **telling**, *los americanos*.

to be bent on be determined

to be intimidated be made to feel afraid

brats *sl.*, ''kids,'' *pej.*

I grew up in a house where the only regular guests were my relations. For one day, enormous families of relatives would visit and there would be so many people that the noise and the bodies would spill out to the backyard and front porch. Then, for weeks, no one came by. (It was usually a salesman who rang the doorbell.) Our house stood apart. A **gaudy** yellow in a row of white **bungalows**. We were the people with the noisy dog. The people who raised pigeons and chickens. We were the foreigners on the block. A few neighbors smiled and waved. We waved back. But no one in the family knew the names of the old couple who lived next door; until I was seven years old, I did not know the names of the kids who lived across the street. . . .

telling here, revealing

los americanos *Sp.*, here, the assimilated people of the United States

gaudy over-bright, over-decorated

bungalow small house

[III] I was a listening child, careful to hear the very different sounds of Spanish and English. Wide-eyed with hearing, I'd listen to sounds more than words. First, there were English (*gringo*) sounds. So many words were still unknown that when the butcher or the lady at the drugstore said something to me, **exotic** polysyllabic sounds would bloom in the midst of their sentences. Often, the speech of people in public seemed to me very loud, booming with confidence. The man behind the counter would literally ask, 'What can I do for you?' But by being so firm and so clear, the sound of his voice said that he was a *gringo*; he belonged in public society. . . .

exotic strange, exciting

I was unable to hear my own sounds, but I knew very well that I spoke English poorly. My words could not stretch far enough to form complete thoughts. And the words I did speak I didn't know well enough to make into distinct sounds. (Listeners would usually lower their heads, better to hear what I was trying to say.) But it was one thing for *me* to speak English with difficulty. It was more troubling for me to hear my parents speak in public. . . .

[IV]   But then there was Spanish. *Español*: my family's   9   *español*   *Sp.*, Spanish
language. *Español*: the language that seemed to me a private language. I'd hear strangers on the radio and in the Mexican Catholic church across town speaking in Spanish, but I couldn't really believe that Spanish was a public language, like English. Spanish speakers, rather, seemed related to me, for I sensed that we shared— through our language—the experience of feeling apart from *los gringos*. It was thus a ghetto* Spanish that I heard and I spoke. . . .

. . . I remained **cloistered** by sounds, timid and shy   **cloistered**   here, sheltered, protected
in public, too dependent on voices at home. And yet it needs to be emphasized: I was an extremely happy child at home. I remember many nights when my father would come back from work, and I'd hear him call out to my mother in Spanish, sounding relieved. In Spanish, he'd sound light and free notes he never could manage in English. Some nights I'd jump up just at hearing his voice. With **mis hermanos** I would come   **mis hermanos**   *Sp.*, my brothers (and sisters)
running into the room where he was with my mother. Our laughing (so deep was the pleasure!) became screaming. Like others who know the pain of public **alienation**, we transformed the knowledge of our public   **alienation**   here, a feeling of separateness, of not belonging
separateness and made it **consoling**—the reminder of   **consoling**   comforting
intimacy. Excited, we joined our voices in a celebration   **intimacy**   feelings of closeness
of sounds. *We are speaking now the way we never speak out in public. We are alone—together,* voices sounded, surrounded to tell me. Some nights, no one seemed willing **to loosen the hold** sounds had on us. At dinner, we   **to loosen the hold**   lessen the power or control
invented new words. (Ours sounded Spanish, but

*ghetto—a part of a city where a group of people live who are poor and not treated as full citizens. Originally, the Jewish quarter of a European city.

made sense only to us.) We **pieced together** new words by taking, say, an English verb and giving it Spanish endings. My mother's instructions at bedtime would be **lacquered** with **mock-urgent** tones. Or a word like *si* would become, in several notes, able to convey added measures of feeling. Tongues explored the edges of words, especially the fat vowels. And we happily sounded that military drum roll, the **twirling** roar of the Spanish *r*. Family language: my family's sounds. The voices of my parents and sisters and brother. Their voices insisting: *You belong here. We are family members. Related. Special to one another. Listen!* Voices singing and sighing, rising, **straining**, then **surging**, **teeming** with pleasure that burst syllables into fragments of laughter. At times it seemed there was steady quiet only when, from another room, the **rustling** whispers of my parents faded and I moved closer to sleep.

[V]   ... my teachers were unsentimental about their [11] responsibility. What they understood was that I needed to speak a public language. So their voices would search me out, asking me questions. Each time I'd hear them, I'd look up in surprise to see a nun's face **frowning** at me. I'd mumble, not really meaning to answer. The nun would persist, 'Richard, stand up. Don't look at the floor. Speak up. Speak to the entire class, not just to me!' But I couldn't believe that the English language was mine to use. (In part, I did not want to believe it.) I continued to mumble. I resisted the teacher's demands. (Did I somehow suspect that once I learned public language my pleasing family life would be changed?) Silent, waiting for the bell to sound, I remained **dazed**, **diffident**, afraid. ...

[VI]   Three months. Five. Half a year passed. Unsmiling, ever watchful, my teachers noted my silence. They began to connect my behavior with the difficult progress my older sister and brother were making. Until one Saturday morning three nuns arrived at the house to talk to our parents. Stiffly, they sat on the blue living room sofa. From the doorway of another room, spying the visitors, I noted the **incongruity**—the **clash** of two worlds, the faces and voices of school **intruding** upon

---

to piece together to put together part by part

lacquered here, covered over in a transparent way

mock-urgent pretending to be urgent

twirling turning in circles

straining pushing or stretching with great effort

surging a forward movement as made by a wave or tide

teeming to be active and bursting with

rustling little sounds caused by touching or rubbing movements

frowning expressing disapproval

dazed confused

diffident timid, shy

incongruity mismatch

clash conflict

intruding entering without permission

the familiar setting of home. I overheard one voice gently wondering, 'Do your children speak only Spanish at home, Mrs. Rodriguez?' While another voice added, 'That Richard especially seems so timid and shy.'

That Rich-heard!   13

With great **tact** the visitors continued, 'Is it possible for you and your husband to encourage your children to practice their English when they are home?' Of course, my parents **complied**. What would they not do for their children's well-being? And how could they have questioned the Church's authority which those women represented? In an instant, they agreed to give up the language (the sounds) that had revealed and accentuated our family's closeness. The moment after the visitors left, the change was observed. *'Ahora*, speak to us *en inglés*,' my father and mother united to tell us. . . .

[VII]   Again and again in the days following, increasingly **15** angry, I was obliged to hear my mother and father: 'Speak to us *en inglés*. (*Speak*.) Only then did I determine to learn classroom English. Weeks after, it happened: One day in school I raised my hand to volunteer an answer. I spoke out in a loud voice. And I did not think it remarkable when the entire class understood. That day, I moved very far from the disadvantaged child I had been only days earlier. The belief, the calming assurance that I belonged in public, had at last **taken hold**.

tact   acting with skill and understanding

to comply   to act in accordance with

ahora   *Sp.*, now

en inglés   *Sp.*, in English

to take hold   here, become established

EXERCISES

A. Understanding the plan

Rodriguez calls *The Hunger of Memory* an autobiography. With this information in mind, what kind of writing would you expect to find in this selection—primarily fictional, primarily factual, or largely impressionistic? (Check again the definitions of *biography*, *autobiography*, and *memoirs* in Chapter 2.) Compare your views before and after reading the material. Notice whether a chronological order is followed.

The subtitle, "The Education of Richard Rodriguez," indicates the specific subject matter of the book. *Subtitles* and *topic headings* are similar: both indicate the specific subject matter included. While subtitles apply to books, articles, plays, or poems, topic headings refer to topic units. A good subtitle or good topic heading fits the material properly. That is, the phrase should not be so broad as to lack focus, but on the other hand, should not be so narrow that it does not cover all the subject matter.

1. To understand this point, look at Section I of the reading with the following topic headings in mind:
   a. The Education of Richard Rodriguez
   b. The Early Education of Richard Rodriguez
   c. The Roman Catholic School That Richard Rodriguez Attended
   d. The English Language Proficiency of Richard Rodriguez at the Time He Entered School
   e. The First Day at School for Richard Rodriguez

What is the problem with (a) and (b) as topic headings? What is the problem with (c) and (d) as topic headings? Does (e) fit well? Could it be worded differently?

Discussion

The problem here is that while (a) may be a good subtitle for the book as a whole, it is too general for Section I. (b) is also too general because the section does not cover the entire early education of the author. (c) is too narrow because the short description of the school is just one of several items discussed. Similarly, (d) is too narrow because the author's knowledge of English is only one item referred to. (d) fits the best of the five suggested headings. The fact that the section is a recollection might be included; the author's name might be excluded since that fact is understood.

2. After you have read the other six sections, match them with the headings that fit best from the list which follows (Then check the Answer Key.):

Headings	*Sections*
Recollection of First Day at School _____	[I] "I remember, to start with, that day in Sacramento . . ."
The Role of Spanish _____	[II] "In the early years of my boyhood . . ."
The Schooling Process _____	[III] "I was a listening child . . ."
The Process Takes Hold _____	[IV] "But then there was Spanish . . ."
Perceptions of Spoken English _____	[V] ". . . my teachers were unsentimental . . ."
Status of Family in the Neighborhood _____	[VI] "Three months. Five. Half a year passed . . ."
Closing the Gap between Home and School _____	[VII] "Again and again in the days following . . ."

3. With a partner, compose a topic heading for the whole selection. Compare your heading with those of other members of the class.

B. Structure practice—Word order: Modifying a whole sentence with an adverb or adjective

Read the last sentence of Section I once again:

"Quickly I turned to see my mother's face dissolve in a watery blur behind the pebbled glass door."

The placement of "quickly" at the beginning of the sentence means that the adverb modifies the whole sentence. If the adverb had been placed close to the verb, then it would modify only the action of "turning":

I turned quickly⎫
⎬ to see my mother's face dissolve in a watery blur behind
I quickly turned⎭ the pebbled glass door.

Read the last paragraph of Section I, noticing the effect of "quickly" placed at the beginning or placed in a medial position in the last sentence. Can you feel the effect of "quickly" at the beginning? Can you feel the interruption of the reporting of what the nun said and did by the boy's sudden realization that his mother was leaving without him?

Here are three other sentences from the selection. Change the beginning adverb or adjective to a medial position. Then read the appropriate part of the selection again. Explain how the difference in word order changes the meaning. With the adjectives you may also have to change the wording.

Example: Laughing, she spoke on the telephone.

She, laughing, spoke on the telephone.
OR
She was laughing when she spoke on the telephone.

1. (Section IV) "Excited, we joined our voices in a celebration of sounds."
    _____
    _____

2. (Section V) "Silent, waiting for the bell to sound, I remained dazed, diffident, afraid." _____
    _____

3. (Section VI) "Stiffly, they sat on the blue living room sofa." _____
    _____

C. Vocabulary practice

Paraphrase the following sentences from the reading in order to make the meaning of the underlined idiom clear. Then use the underlined idiom in a sentence of your own.

Example: It took some time until I got a hold on the subject matter.

Paraphrase: **It took a little while until I got some understanding and control of the ideas in the material.**

New Sentence: **How long do you think it will take before you get a hold on your new work?**

1. "Nor was the Sacramento of the fifties <u>bent on</u> teaching them a contrary lesson."

   Paraphrase: _____

   _____

   New Sentence: _____

   _____

2. "Some nights, no one seemed willing <u>to loosen the hold</u> sounds had on us."

   Paraphase: _____

   _____

   New Sentence: _____

   _____

3. "We <u>pieced together</u> new words by taking, say, an English verb and giving it Spanish endings."

   Paraphrase: _____

   _____

   New Sentence: _____

   _____

4. "The belief, the calming assurance that I belonged in public, had at last <u>taken hold</u>."

   Paraphrase: _____

   _____

   New Sentence: _____

   _____

D. Understanding the ideas (for oral or written discussion)

1. An important concept to Rodriguez is the *difference between public and private language*. What do you think he means by public and private language? Which was his public language? Which was his private language? Do you think one can have a public language and a private language even if that person knows only a single language?

2. *A sense of alienation* and *a sense of belonging* is another contrast which concerned Rodriguez. Alienation is a feeling of separatedness, apartness, aloneness. It is a feeling of not being wanted or included in one social group or another. (a) Did the parents feel a sense of alienation in Sacramento? (b) Did the family feel alienated in their neighborhood? (c) Did Richard have a sense of alienation when he first entered school? Find a passage in the reading to use in explaining your answer to each of these questions.

3. At the school, one of the nuns said to the young boy,

   "Richard, stand up. Don't look at the floor. Speak up. Speak to the entire class, not just to me!"

The nun expressed some of the *cultural expectations* for behavior in an American classroom. Think about your early education. What kind of behavior did your elementary school teachers expect from you? For example, did they expect you to stand up when you answered a question they asked? Did they expect you to address the whole class? Was this true from the earliest grades? What was different from the description given here?

4. The reading continues to the point where Rodriguez <u>did</u> "speak up" in class. What elements contributed to his ability to participate in this way?

5. Rodriguez writes from the point of view of someone of Mexican background who was born in the United States. Those from other Latin American backgrounds or social groups may have quite different points of view. If you are from Latin America or your background is Latin American, try to explain your reactions to Rodriguez's experience. Would people from your cultural group react the way Rodriguez did in school, at home, at the drugstore, toward *los otros*, that is, toward those outside their own cultural group? Let class members from other culture areas ask you questions.

E. Topics for comparison of Chapter 2, *Mount Allegro*, and Chapter 3, *The Hunger of Memory*

1. Compare the school situations *depicted* or described by Mangione and Rodriguez. Consider the *make-up* or composition of the student body, whether the school was public or private, and the attitude of the parents towards the teachers.

2. Compare the attitudes toward speaking the native language and speaking English at home as the two authors describe them. How did these attitudes help or *hinder*, that is, make difficult, the process of acculturation? (Refer again to Chapter 2, definition of Acculturation.)

3. In both *Mount Allegro* and *The Hunger of Memory*, the family unit is strong, important, and close. However, the family units differed in some respects. Choose the adjectives which would best describe the attitudes of the families.

Family in Mount Allegro	*Adjectives*	*Family in* The Hunger of Memory
————————————	humble	————————————
————————————	complying	————————————
————————————	defiant /di-ˈfī-ant/	————————————
————————————	independent	————————————
————————————	gentle	————————————
————————————	understanding	————————————
————————————	patient	————————————
————————————	cloistered	————————————
————————————	respectful	————————————
————————————	musical	————————————

Write a paragraph explaining your choices.

F. Optional exercises

1. Suppose Miss Zimmerman, the teacher in *Mount Allegro*, came to the Amoroso household and suggested to the parents that they speak to their children in English. What do you think the parents' response would have been?

Role Playing Activity

Let one person act the part of Miss Zimmerman, and let others act Mr. and Mrs. Amoroso, Gerlando, Uncle Luigi, and Uncle Nino. Have Miss Zimmerman come to the house to discuss the matter of speaking English. Imagine how the family would behave while she was there, and then what they would say after she left.

2. Suppose the relatives in *The Hunger of Memory* returned for a second visit at a late hour on a Sunday evening for a *sirinata* as was done in *Mount Allegro*. How would the Rodriguez family have felt? How do you imagine the various neighbors would have reacted?

Role Playing Activity

Let some people act as the neighbors, some as the relatives, and some as Mr. and Mrs. Rodriguez. Act out the following sequence of events: (a) the relatives returning for a *sirinata*; (b) Mr. and Mrs. Rodriguez coming to the door, at first feeling unsure, but then welcoming the family again; (c) then, some neighbors telephoning or knocking at the door. Act out the situation saying what you think the various characters would say.

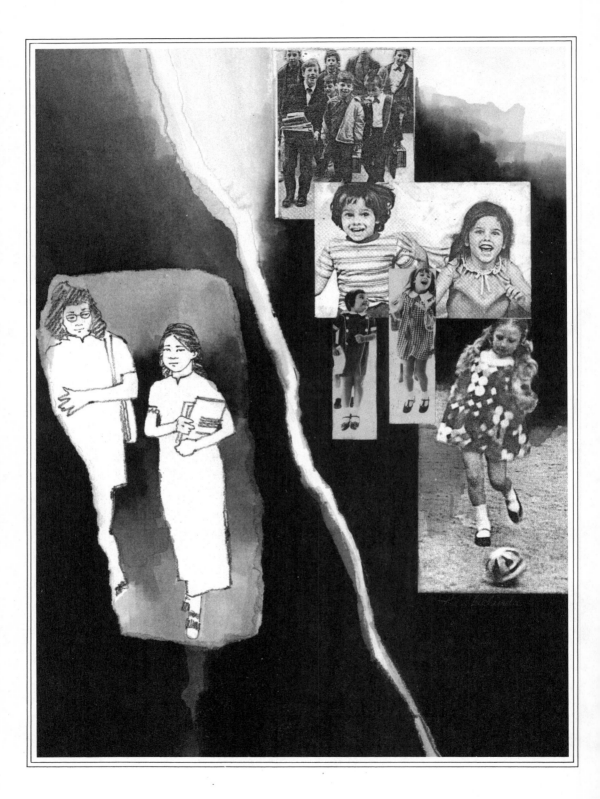

4

MAXINE HONG KINGSTON

from *The Woman Warrior: Memoirs of a Girlhood among Ghosts*

Maxine Hong Kingston (b. 1940), the daughter of Chinese immigrants, was born and raised in Stockton, California, and received her higher education at the University of California, Berkeley. A writer and teacher, she now lives in Honolulu with her husband and son.

The book from which our selection is taken, *The Woman Warrior**: *Memoirs of a Girlhood among Ghosts*† (1976), won the general non-fiction award of the National Book Critics Circle.[1] Like Rodriguez, Kingston was also a youngster whose native language was not English. She also faced the problem of speaking up in English in school. She too was trying to establish her own sense of identity. Keep in mind the title and subtitle as you read. What kind of battle is this warrior fighting? Who is the enemy? Who are the ghosts?

*warrior—a literary term for an experienced soldier or long-time fighter for his tribe or cause (Note: to make this term feminine, the word "woman" is added. You can say "actor" or "actress," but for clarity you add "woman" for a "woman garage mechanic," "a woman warrior," or other traditionally male occupations.).

†ghosts—phantoms (The author's mother referred to all people other than those of Chinese descent as "ghosts.").

[1]The National Book Critics Circle (founded in 1974) gives annual awards in four categories—non-fiction, fiction, poetry, and criticism—for books written in English by American authors.

from The Woman Warrior

... When I went to kindergarten and had to 1 speak English for the first time, I became silent. A dumbness — a shame — still cracks my voice in two, even when I want to say "hello" casually, or ask an easy question in front of the **check-out counter**, or ask directions of a bus driver. I stand frozen, or I **hold up the line** with the complete, grammatical sentence that comes **squeaking** out at impossible length. "What did you say?" says the cab driver, or "Speak up," so I have to perform again, only weaker the second time. A telephone call makes my throat bleed and takes up that day's courage. It spoils my day with self-disgust when I hear my broken voice come **skittering** out into the open. It makes people **wince** to hear it. I'm getting better, though. Recently I asked the postman for special-issue stamps*; I've waited since childhood for postmen to give me some **of their own accord**. I am making progress, a little every day.

My silence was thickest — total — during the three years that I covered my school paintings with black paint. I painted layers of black over houses and flowers and suns, and when I drew on the blackboard, I put a layer of chalk on top. I was making a stage curtain, and it was the moment before the curtain parted or rose. The teachers called my parents to school, and I saw they had been saving my pictures, curling and cracking, all alike and black. The teachers pointed to the pictures and looked serious, talked seriously too, but my parents did not understand English. ("The parents and teachers of criminals were executed," said my father.) My parents took the pictures home. I spread them out (so black and full of possibilities) and pretended the curtains were swinging open, flying up, one after another, sunlight underneath, mighty operas.

During the first silent year I spoke to no one at 3

check-out counter   here, counter where you pay for purchases

to hold up the line   delay the line of people

squeaking   a high, mouselike noise

to skitter   move quickly over the surface

to wince   make a quick movement in reaction to pain

of their own accord   here, without being asked

*special-issue stamps—postage stamps to mark special events or famous people.

school, did not ask before going to the lavatory, and **flunked** kindergarten. My sister also said nothing for three years, silent in the playground and silent at lunch. There were other quiet Chinese girls not of our family, but most of them got over it sooner than we did. I enjoyed the silence. At first it did not occur to me I was supposed to talk or to pass kindergarten. I talked at home and to one or two of the Chinese kids in class. I made motions and even made some jokes. I drank out of a toy saucer when the water spilled out of the cup, and everybody laughed, pointing at me, so I did it some more. I didn't know that Americans don't drink out of saucers.

  I liked the Negro students (Black Ghosts) best because they laughed the loudest and talked to me as if I were a **daring** talker too. One of the Negro girls had her mother **coil braids** over her ears Shanghai-style like mine; we were Shanghai twins except that she was covered with black like my paintings. Two Negro kids enrolled in Chinese school, and the teachers gave them Chinese names. Some Negro kids walked me to school and home, protecting me from the Japanese kids, who hit me and chased me and stuck gum in my ears. The Japanese kids were noisy and tough. They appeared one day in kindergarten, released from concentration camp,* which was a tic-tac-toe† mark, like **barbed wire**, on the map.

  It was when I found out I had to talk that school 5 became a misery, that the silence became a misery. I did not speak and felt bad each time that I did not speak. I read aloud in first grade, though, and heard the **barest** whisper with little squeaks come out of my throat. "Louder," said the teacher, who scared the voice away again. The other Chinese girls did not talk either, so I knew the silence had to do with being a Chinese girl.

to flunk *sl.*, fail, as an exam

daring very brave
to coil form into a circle
braid several bands of hair or thread put together to make a thicker band

barbed wire wire with short, sharp points on it, used for fences

barest least possible amount

*concentration camp—during World War II, Americans of Japanese descent were forced to live in special areas or internment camps.

†tic-tac-toe—children's game. In this game, one player's mark is "X" and the other player's mark is "O." They take turns putting their marks in the spaces formed by a grid that looks like this: ╫ . The winner has three "O's" and "X's" in a vertical, horizontal, or diagonal line (In *Br. Eng.* called "noughts and crosses.").

Reading out loud was easier than speaking because we did not have to make up what to say, but I stopped often, and the teacher would think I'd gone quiet again. I could not understand "**I**." The Chinese "I" has seven **strokes, intricacies**. How could the American "I," assuredly wearing a hat like the Chinese, have only three strokes, the middle so straight? Was it out of politeness that this writer left off strokes the way a Chinese has to write her own name small and crooked? No, it was not politeness; "I" is a capital and "you" is lower-case. I stared at that middle line and waited so long for its black center to resolve into tight strokes and dots that I forgot to pronounce it. The other troublesome word was "**here**," no strong consonant to hang on to, and so flat, when "here" is two mountainous **ideographs**. The teacher, who had already told me every day how to read "I" and "here," put me in the low corner under the stairs again, where the noisy boys usually sat.

When my second grade class did a play, the whole 7 class went to the auditorium except the Chinese girls. The teacher, lovely and Hawaiian, should have understood about us, but instead left us behind in the classroom. Our voices were too soft or nonexistent, and our parents never signed the permission slips anyway. They never signed anything unnecessary. We opened the door a crack and **peeked** out, but closed it again quickly. One of us (not me) won every **spelling bee**, though.

I remember telling the Hawaiian teacher, "We Chinese can't sing 'land where our fathers died.' " She argued with me about politics, while I meant because of **curses**. But how can I have that memory when I couldn't talk? My mother says that we, like the ghosts, have no memories.

After American school, we picked up our cigar 9 boxes, in which we had arranged books, brushes, and an inkbox neatly, and went to Chinese school,* from 5:00 to 7:30 P.M. There we chanted together, voices rising

strokes   here, pen or brush marks

intricate   *adj.*, having many interrelated, complicated parts

I

ideograph   written character symbolizing a whole idea, such as those used in Chinese writing

here

to peek   look quickly
spelling bee   spelling contest

curses   misfortune ordered by high or supernatural authority

*Chinese school—Parents often send their children to after-school "schools" where religion or the language and customs of the family's background are taught. Like Chinese school, one can find Hebrew school, Greek school, and so on.

and falling, loud and soft, some boys shouting, everybody reading together, reciting together and not alone with one voice. When we had a memorization test, the teacher let each of us come to his desk and say the lesson to him privately, while the rest of the class practiced copying or tracing. Most of the teachers were men. The boys who were so well behaved in the American school played tricks on them and **talked back** to them. The girls were not **mute**. They screamed and yelled during recess, when there were no rules; they had **fist**-fights. Nobody was afraid of children hurting themselves or of children hurting school property. The glass doors to the red and green balconies with the gold joy symbols were left wide open so that we could run out and climb the fire escapes. We played **capture-the-flag** in the auditorium, where Sun Yat-sen and Chiang Kai-shek's pictures hung at the back of the stage, the Chinese flag on their left and the American flag on their right. We climbed the **teak** ceremonial chairs and made flying leaps off the stage. One flag headquarters was behind the glass door and the other on stage right. Our feet drummed on the hollow stage. During recess the teachers locked themselves up in their office with the shelves of books, copybooks, inks from China. They drank tea and warmed their hands at a stove. There was no play supervision. At recess we had the school to ourselves, and also we could roam as far as we could go—downtown, Chinatown stores, home—as long as we returned before the bell rang.

At exactly 7:30 the teacher again picked up the brass bell that sat on his desk and swung it over our heads, while we charged down the stairs, our cheering magnified in the stairwell. Nobody had to line up.

to talk back answer disrespectfully

mute silent

fist fingers closed tightly to form ball shape

capture-the-flag a children's game

teak kind of wood

EXERCISES

A. Understanding the plan—Chronological or topical organization

We have studied chronological order (see Chapter 1) as an organizing principle for a piece of writing. We saw in Chapter 1, "The Summer of the Beautiful White Horse," that what happened first, then next, and next, and so on was very important in the unfolding of the story. Again, in Chapter 3, *The Hunger of Memory*, the progression from the first day of school until the day that young Richard first spoke up in class traces his development, step by step, chronologically.

What about chronological order as the organizing principle in this selection? Is the material arranged in chronological order? If so, what *time span*, that is, what period of time, does this reading cover? To find the answer to these questions, *scan*, that is, go quickly through each paragraph to pick out only the references to time periods.

Note the phrase from each paragraph that indicates a specific period of time, following the example for paragraph 1:

Paragraph	Phrase
1	"When I went to kindergarten . . ."
2	
3	
5	
7	

What time span does the selection cover? (Check the Answer Key.)

Is the subject matter really organized by this time span? Look again at the sentences in which you found the time phrases above. Notice that each time phrase indicates another topic. Then read the selection straight through with the following headings in mind and decide which one tells best what the piece is really about:

1. The First Three Years of Schools

2. The Difference between American Public Schools and Chinese After-School

3. The Inability to Speak English

4. The Belief That Silence Is Golden

5. The Attempt to Overcome Silence in an English-speaking Environment

While the author does use a time frame, at a more basic level the piece centers around the author's attempts to overcome silence in an English-speaking environment. She gives us various *recollections*, or memories and associations relating to this topic. You can find further illustrations of this kind of organization, that is, this *topical order*, by studying paragraph 1.

B. Structural focus—Choice of tense in paragraph 1

The first sentence in paragraph 1 indicates the starting point of the author's silence, and therefore uses the past tense: "When I <u>went</u> to kindergarten . . . I <u>became</u> silent." The next sentence expresses the author's typical reactions when certain situations recur, and therefore uses the simple present tense: "A dumbness—a shame—still <u>cracks</u> my voice in two, even when I <u>want</u> to say 'hello' casually, or ask an easy question, or. . . ." Sentences 3–7 describe some of her other attempts to overcome silence, and thus they continue in the simple present tense. Sentence 8 reports ongoing improvement with the present continuous tense. Sentence 9 gives a recent example of this improvement by describing the incident with the postman. A combination of simple past and present perfect tenses serves to place this incident in the recent past. In the final sentence, the writer reinforces the idea introduced in sentence 8 by using the present continuous tense again: "I <u>am</u> <u>making</u> progress, a little every day."

Exercise Practice

With this review of tense choice in mind, look at the following paragraph. Try to explain the intention of each sentence together with the choice of tenses.

(1) One day when I was five years old, I became afraid of dogs. (2) That day, a huge black dog ran towards me barking loudly, and bit the sleeve of my coat. (3) A cold sweat still comes over me whenever I see even a small black dog or hear the bark of a dog in the far distance. (4) I stand frozen even before a playful little puppy and feel ashamed when the owner says, "He won't hurt you." (5) I insult dog owners who would like me to admire their pets. (6) It spoils my day when I try to pat a small dog and see my hand pull back before I touch the animal. (7) I am improving, however. (8) The other day, I stood close to a sleeping dog and admired its clean and shiny fur. (9) So you see, I am making progress.

C. Pronunciation practice—Phrases for rhythm, stress, and pitch

You should practice the following phrases from the reading individually, in sentences, and in the context of the text.

1. Read these explanations of rhythm, stress, and pitch symbols. Then practice saying the phrases which follow and note particularly their rhythm, stress, and pitch.

Rhythm:
    long sound = ♩
    short sound = ♪

Stress:
    primary stress = ´
    secondary stress = ´

Pitch:
As shown in the diagram, the arrow approximates English pitch. (The X's represent
    words.)
Arrowhead points <u>downward</u> to Pitch <u>1</u>.
Arrow line just <u>below</u> printed word is at Pitch <u>2</u>.
Arrow line just <u>above</u> printed word is at Pitch <u>3</u>.
Arrow line at some points goes slightly above Pitch 3 in the direction of Pitch <u>4</u>.

Pitch 4
Pitch 3
Pitch 2 ⟨X   X   X   X
Pitch 1

Your instructor may model the phrases while tapping out the rhythm.

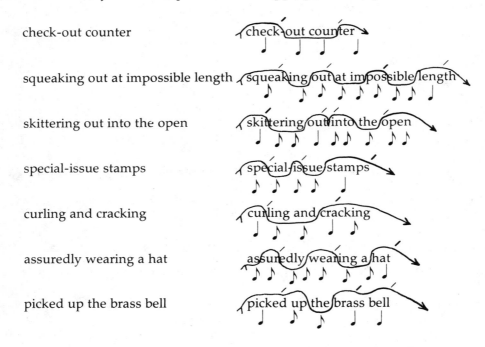

check-out counter

squeaking out at impossible length

skittering out into the open

special-issue stamps

curling and cracking

assuredly wearing a hat

picked up the brass bell

2. Seven sentence starters appear in the following left column. Match each one with the appropriate phrase on the right. Check your answer by having one person read aloud the starter and another complete the sentence. The instructor should check your pronunciation. (See the Answer Key if necessary.)

(a) Going to church she was	(1) check-out counter.
(b) The burning wood in the fireplace was	(2) squeaking out at impossible length.
(c) We paid for the food at the	(3) skittering out into the open.
(d) When she played the violin, the sound came	(4) special-issue stamps.
(e) The ball bounced and went	(5) curling and cracking.
(f) Although it was heavy, he	(6) assuredly wearing a hat.
(g) I went to the post office to buy some	(7) picked up the brass bell.

3. Find the correct phrase in the selection and then read the entire sentence aloud, as your instructor requests.

D. Understanding the ideas

The author's method is to select and present incidents which throw light on her topic. From these descriptions, as readers, we must piece together the author's home and school situation and the extremely difficult acculturation process she experienced.

1. How do her feelings about being silent in school change during those early years?
   a. How does she feel about being silent <u>before</u> she finds out that she has to talk in school? (Refer to paragraph 3)
   b. How does she feel <u>after</u> she realizes this fact? (Refer to paragraph 5)
   c. How does she feel <u>now</u>, that is, at the moment of writing? (Refer to paragraph 1)

Since the selection of incidents is very important to the author's purpose, let us examine three of them closely and see how they relate to the central issue.

2. Incident in Paragraph 2: In this paragraph, the author says, "My silence was thickest—total—during the three years that I covered my school paintings with black paint." Summarize the incident that she describes.
   a. How does she justify the black paint she puts over her paintings and the layer of chalk she puts over her blackboard drawings?
   b. What do her teachers do?
   c. How do her parents react?
   d. How would you explain her spreading out the pictures at home?

3. Incident in Paragraph 3: In this paragraph, we have a description of the author's kindergarten year. How would you *characterize* or explain the nature of her experience? Do you find any humor there? Use some appropriate adjectives. Include your *interpretation* or explanation of the incident with the toy saucers.

4. Incident in Paragraph 6: Describe the problem that the author has with the English word "I." What does she mean when she says (paragraph 6),

   > I stared at that middle line and waited so long for its black center to resolve into tight strokes and dots that I forgot to pronounce it.

   Have you ever had a similar kind of experience with English and your own language?

5. Choose three of the following qualities and, using examples, indicate how each describes the author's state of mind at a particular point. For example, take the quality of "shame." When does the author feel this way? What are the circumstances? Does this feeling change over the course of time?

shame	stubbornness	self-disgust*	intelligence
courage	disobedience	fright	obedience
dumbness	humor	enjoyment	bewilderment†

*self-disgust—self-distaste.
†bewilderment—confusion.

6. Compare the behavior of the Chinese-American children in public school and in Chinese After-School. If you were born and raised in a Chinese-speaking culture, please comment on the school situations presented in the reading.

E. Topics for discussion and comparison

Concept Vocabulary

1. The meaning of *explicit* versus *implicit*.
   Something *explicit* is something clearly and fully expressed. On the other hand, something *implicit* is something strongly suggested but not directly described or explained.
   a. Consider this quote from Richard Rodriguez in Chapter 3:

   > My teachers were unsentimental about their responsibility. What they understood was that I needed to speak a public language.

   Is it an example of an explicit or implicit expression of an idea?
   b. Now look at this passage from Maxine Hong Kingston:

   > I read aloud in first grade, though, and heard the barest whisper with little squeaks come out of my throat. "Louder," said the teacher, who scared the voice away again.

   What emotion is young Maxine feeling? Would you say that her teacher is "unsentimental about [her] responsibility," understanding that what the child needs is "to speak a public language"?
   Is it an example of explicit or implicit writing? Rewrite this passage making it as explicit as you can.

2. The concept of *culture shock*.
   The term *culture shock* has come into common use within the last twenty-five years or so. "Culture" here means the particular system of art, thought, and customs of a society, such as Chinese culture, French culture, and so on. A "shock" is a sudden blow or disturbance to the body, the mind, or the emotions. Thus *culture shock* refers to the strong effect an individual experiences when placed in a completely unfamiliar environment.[2]
   a. Richard Rodriguez doesn't have an easy time adjusting to school; however, his difficulties are not as great as those of Maxine Hong Kingston. We know that both of them are sensitive and intelligent and that they wish to do well. How would you account for the difference in their rate of adjustment to the culture?
      In your answer, take into consideration the role of the parents: their knowledge of English, their attitude toward teachers and school authorities, the kind of example they set, and so on.

[2]For definition of "culture shock" see Alvin Toffler, *Future Shock* (New York: Random House, 1970), pp. 308–309. See also earlier definition by psychologist Sven Lundstedt, "Personality Determinants and Assessments," *Journal of Social Issues*, 19 (1963), 3.

Panel for Role Play (Optional Activity): Attitude toward Those Outside of One's Cultural Group

In Mangione's "world," the outsiders are *Americani*; in Rodriguez' world, they are called *los gringos* or *los americanos*; in Kingston's setting they are referred to as "ghosts."

Pretend that the parents in *Mount Allegro*, *The Hunger of Memory*, and *The Woman Warrior* are able to explain their views toward American people as a whole. What would they say? Set up a panel of six class members so that both parents from each "world" are represented. Have each panel member state his or her position. Have the rest of the class make up questions to ask Mr. Amoroso, Mrs. Rodriguez, or Mr. Hong and the others. Select a moderator to introduce the subject, call on the panel members, and ask for questions from the class.

5

THOMAS S. WHITECLOUD

from "Blue Winds Dancing"

Thomas S. Whitecloud (1914–1972) was a native American Indian who spent much of his youth on the Lac du Flambeau Chippewa Reservation[1] in Wisconsin. After a troubled boyhood, during which he was *expelled from*, that is, required to leave, several Indian schools, he finally decided on medicine as a career. Working hard to raise his grades for admission to medical school, he first attended the University of New Mexico and later graduated from the University of Redlands in California. In 1939, he entered the Tulane University Medical School.

As a physician, Dr. Whitecloud worked for a time with the Indian Service of the government, and then established a private practice in Texas, where for more than seven years he was the only doctor in an entire county. After his retirement, Dr. Whitecloud was instrumental in establishing the American Association of Indian Physicians.

"Blue Winds Dancing" won the first prize in a Phi Beta Kappa[2] essay contest in 1938. It was published in *Scribner's Magazine* in February 1939. The author wrote it while he was at college in Southern California. The passage reprinted here is written in the form of an *interior monologue*. In this form, a writer tries to record certain thoughts and associations as they occur. Sometimes, in the desire to reveal this interior flow of thoughts, the writer does not follow grammatical rules exactly.

[1]The U.S. government set aside certain sections of land, or *reservations*, and required native American Indians to live there. The Bureau of Indian Affairs, an agency of the government, administered these reservations as well as the special schools set up for American Indians. Today, American Indians are American citizens, and therefore they may live, work, and study where they wish. The historically troubled relationship between American Indians and the U.S. government is explained well in the article "American Indians, Federal Policy Towards" by Edward H. Spicer which appears in the *Harvard Encyclopedia of American Ethnic Groups*, ed. Stephan Thernstrom (Cambridge: Harvard Univ. Press, 1980), pp. 114–122. Also, see Dee A. Brown, *Bury My Heart at Wounded Knee: An Indian History of the American West* (New York: Holt, Rinehart & Winston, 1971).
[2]Phi Beta Kappa, pronounced /fi/ /ˈbāt-ə/ /ˈkap-ə/, is a national honor society, founded in 1776, whose members are chosen for lifetime membership from among college undergraduates of high academic achievement.

from Blue Winds Dancing

There is a moon out tonight. Moon and stars and 1
clouds tipped with moonlight. And there is a fall
wind blowing in my heart. Ever since this evening, when against a fading sky I saw geese **wedge**
southward. They were going home. . . . Now I try to
study, but against the pages I see them again, driving
southward. Going home.

wedge   here, to travel in a V-shaped formation

Across the valley there are heavy mountains holding up the night sky, and beyond the mountains there is
home. Home, and peace, and the beat of drums, and
blue winds dancing over snow fields. The Indian lodge
will fill with my people, and our gods will come and
sit among them. I should be there then. I should be
at home.

But home is beyond the mountains, and I am here. 3
Here where fall hides in the valleys and winter never
comes down from the mountains. Here where all the
trees grow in rows; the **palms** stand stiffly by the roadsides, and in the groves the oranges trees line in military
rows and endlessly bear fruit. Beautiful, yes; there is
always beauty in order, in rows of growing things! But it
is the beauty of captivity. A **pine** fighting for existence
on a windy **knoll** is much more beautiful.

palm   tree with fanlike leaves found in warm climates

pine   tree with needlelike leaves which stay green year round

knoll   small hill

In my Wisconsin, the leaves change before the
snows come. In the air there is the smell of wild rice and
venison cooking; and when the winds come whispering
through the forests, they carry the smell of rotting
leaves. In the evenings, the **loon** calls, lonely; and birds
sing their last songs before leaving. Bears dig roots and
eat late fall berries, fattening for their long winter sleep.
Later, when the first snows fall, one awakens in the
morning to find the world white and beautiful and
clean. Then one can look back over his **trail** and see the
tracks following. In the woods there are tracks of deer
and snowshoe rabbits and long **streaks** where **par-
tridges slide** to **alight**. **Chipmunks** make tiny footprints
on the **limbs**; and one can hear squirrels busy in the

venison   deer meat

loon   large diving bird that eats fish; has a wild cry

trail   line or mark left by a passerby

tracks   here, footprints

streaks   long, thin lines

partridge   middle-sized bird

to slide   move over a polished surface

to alight   land on

chipmunk   small striped squirrel-like animal

limbs   here, large branches

hollow trees, sorting **acorns**. Soft lake waves wash the shores, and sunsets burst each evening over the lakes and make them look as if they were **afire**.

That land which is my home! Beautiful, calm— where there is no hurry to get anywhere, no driving to keep up in a race that knows no ending and no goal. No classes where men talk and talk, and then stop now and then to hear their own words come back to them from the students. No constant **peering** into the **maelstrom** of one's mind; no worries about grades and honors; no **hysterical** preparing for life until that life is half over; no anxiety about one's place in the thing they call Society.

I hear again the ring of axes in deep woods, the **crunch** of snow beneath my feet. I feel again the smooth velvet of ghost-**birch bark**. I hear the rhythm of the drums. . . . I am tired. I am weary of trying to keep up this **bluff** of being civilized. Being civilized means trying to do everything you don't want to, never doing anything you want to. It means dancing to the strings of custom and tradition; it means living in houses and never knowing or caring who is next door. These civilized white men want us to be like them—always dissatisfied, getting a hill and wanting a mountain.

Then again, maybe I am not tired. Maybe I'm **licked**. Maybe I am just not smart enough to **grasp** these things that go to make up civilization. Maybe I am just too lazy to think hard enough to keep up.

Still, I know my people have many things that civilization has taken from the whites. They know how to give, how to tear one man's piece of meat in two and share it with one's brother. They know how to sing— how to make each man his own songs and sing them; for their music they do not have to listen to other men singing over a radio. They know how to make things with their hands, how to shape beads into design and make a thing of beauty from a piece of birch bark.

But we are inferior. It is terrible to have to feel inferior, to have to read reports of intelligence tests and learn that one's race is behind. It is terrible to sit in classes and hear men tell you that your people **worship** sticks of wood—that your gods are all false, that the

acorns   oak tree seeds

afire   on fire

peering   observing closely
maelstrom   whirlpool
hysterical   emotionally uncontrolled

crunch   a noisy crushing
birch   tree with smooth gray bark
bark   outer layer of a tree
bluff   pretense

licked   *inf.*, defeated
to grasp   hold firmly; here, understand fully

to worship   pray to

Manitou forgot your people and did not write them a   **Manitou** Great Spirit
book.*

I am tired. I want to walk again among the ghost-
birches. I want to see the leaves turn in autumn, the
smoke rise from the lodgehouses, and to feel the blue
winds. I want to hear the drums; I want to hear the
drums and feel the blue whispering winds. . . .

*Whitecoud is probably referring to a book such as the Bible or the Koran.

EXERCISES

A. Understanding the plan—Paragraph 1: Setting the frame

In paragraph 1 the author sets the whole direction of the piece. We learn where he is,
what he is doing, what has specifically caused his mind to wander from his work, and where
he longs to be. He has *conveyed* or communicated this information without precisely following the rules of sentence construction. When writers write in this way to create a special
impression, we say that they are using *poetic license*.

For example, take the last two words of paragraph 1 (vii), "Going home." Grammati-
cally, they do not form a complete sentence. However, Whitecloud intends to create a deep
impression with them, as though he had underlined the two words. They bring together the
important information of the paragraph that (a) the geese in the sky are going home; (b) the
narrator wishes that he were going home too; and (c) he will tell the reader in the succeeding
paragraphs some of the reasons for his intense longing to go home and to be home.

B. Structure focus—Sentence fragments

Throughout the selection you will notice that there are a number of *sentence fragments*,
that is, incomplete sentences. They are examples of the poetic license explained in A. Some
sentence fragments may consist of a subject but no verb; some may be the other way around,
with no subject; still others may contain just a dependent clause or simply a phrase. (See
paragraph 1 which follows.)

> (i) There is a moon out tonight. (ii) Moon and stars and clouds tipped with
> moonlight. (iii) And there is a fall wind blowing in my heart. (iv) Ever since
> this evening, when against a fading sky I saw geese wedge southward. (v)
> They were going home. . . . (vi) Now I try to study, but against the pages I
> see them again, driving southward. (vii) Going home.

The first clause (i) is a complete sentence. The second item (ii) is a sentence fragment because
it has no verb. We, as readers, must understand that the author intends to add on to the
subject of (i) and share its verb. Thus, not only is there a "moon out tonight" but also "stars"
and "clouds tipped with moonlight." What else is happening tonight? If in (iii) you consider
"and" to mean "also," or "at the same time," then you have a second complete sentence,

"there is a fall wind blowing in my heart." Taking items (i), (ii), and (iii) together, we see what is outside and what is inside the author's heart.

Clauses (v) and (vi) are complete sentences. We know the geese are going home and that the author is trying to study. What is the meaning of "against the pages I see them again, driving southward"? It could have both *literal* and *figurative* meanings.[3] In the literal sense, perhaps the shadow the flying geese make is moving across the pages of the narrator's book. In the figurative sense, perhaps in the narrator's mind instead of seeing the words on the pages he sees geese flying southward. Can you think of other literal or figurative meanings? Item (vii) is a closing phrase which strongly suggests and sums up the topic.

Exercise for Structure Focus

We have studied the complete sentences and the sentence fragments in paragraph 1. With this background in mind, complete the sentence fragments in paragraphs 2–5 so that they follow the author's meaning.

Paragraph 2:
Sentence Fragment: "Home, and peace, and the beat of drums, and blue winds dancing over snow fields."
Complete Sentence: _____

_____

Paragraph 3:
Sentence Fragment: "Here where fall hides in the valleys and winter never comes down from the mountains."
Complete Sentence: _____

_____

Sentence Fragment: "Here where all the trees grow in rows; the palms stand stiffly by the roadsides, and in the groves the orange trees line in military rows and endlessly bear fruit."
Complete Sentence: _____

_____

Paragraph 4:
All the sentences are complete.

Paragraph 5:
There is one complete sentence in the paragraph. Which sentence is it? Write out the remaining sentence fragments and make complete sentences of them by adding the appropriate information.

[3]literal and figurative meanings—To explain these two aspects of meaning, consider the word "heart." The heart of the body is the single most important organ, the one that pumps blood to all parts of the body. When we speak of the heart of a problem, we mean the most important part that affects everything else. A body *literally* has a heart; a problem *figuratively* has a heart.

C. Language focus—Repetition of words and phrases and use of parallel structure for emphasis and clarity

In paragraphs 1 and 2, the constructions "there is" and "there are" are used four times and, although not stated explicitly, are understood in several sentence fragments. This relatively simple repetition lays out a relationship between the moon, the wind, and the author's heart and home. In paragraph 3, he repeats the words "here where" twice in parallel fashion. How do the two bits of information given after these words relate to each other and contrast with the other information found in the paragraph?

In paragraph 4, what other repetitions of the phrase type "in my Wisconsin" do you find? How do the bits of information given after these words relate to each other?

What is a dominant phrase type in paragraph 5? What negative contrasts does the author make with his sense of his home? What strong criticisms is he making?

In paragraph 6, we have three sets of repeated phrases. The first includes "I hear again," "I feel again." What do the second and third sets of repeated phrases include? How do you explain their relationship to each other?

Paragraph 7 picks up the second set of repeated phrases from paragraph 6. Notice how the simple tiredness that the author expressed in paragraph 6 changes here to *self-condemnation* or self-blame. He blames himself in three ways. What are they?

Paragraph 8 has another set of parallel sentences. To which topic do they all relate? What points does Whitecloud make?

Paragraph 9 has a set of two parallel sentences, each starting with a very strong phrase. What is the phrase? Can you make a connection between the feelings the author shows here and those of self-condemnation present in paragraph 6?

Finally, in paragraph 10, the repeated language seems to express an affirmative desire. Do you understand more clearly now what the phrase "Going home" in the first paragraph means?

D. Understanding the plan—Development of the theme

From the study of the repeated phrases and sentence types in C, we can see the connection between language and *theme*, or main idea. In good writing, the form also supports the theme. The form of interior monologue applies to the selection as a whole. We can apply it even more specifically to paragraphs 5–10. In these six paragraphs we see a discussion going on inside the author as if he were participating in a debate. He is comparing the beliefs and customs of the white man's society with those of his people. How do these two societies differ? What conclusions does the author reach?

Exercise

Write a composition of about three paragraphs in the form of an interior monologue. Use some repeated words or structures in each paragraph, and give some conclusions in the last paragraph. Your theme may be your feelings about "going home," or you may choose another topic about which you have strong feelings.

E. Topics for discussion

1. Review the difference between assimilation and acculturation as discussed in Chapter 2. Do you believe that Whitecloud was assimilated or acculturated at the time he wrote "Blue Winds Dancing"? Explain your answer.

2. What is the author's view of competition in society? Refer especially to paragraphs 5–8.

3. What is his view of his fellow men?

4. Go through the selection again underlining all the references to nature. How would you describe Whitecloud's attitude toward nature? Consider the following issues:

   a. Should human beings *exploit* nature; that is, should they use nature for any purpose convenient to them?

   b. Are human beings a part of nature? If so, should they not be seeking a harmonious relationship to nature?

   c. Can *inanimate* or non-living parts of nature take on an active, living quality? Look especially at the author's description of the "mountains holding up the night sky" in paragraph 2 and the activity of the sunsets in paragraph 3.

5. In the final paragraph, Whitecloud says that he wants to *see*, wants to *hear*, wants to *feel*. What other references to physical senses can you find in the selection? What value do you think the author places on using the senses?

6

TOSHIO MORI

"The Woman Who Makes Swell Doughnuts"

from *Yokohama, California*

Toshio Mori (1910–1980) was born of Japanese immigrant parents and lived for most of his life in California. As perhaps the first major Japanese-American writer of fiction, his work spanned a period of over forty-five years. A resident and observer of the Oakland–San Leandro area of California, Mori succeeded in "capturing the *milieu** of what it was like to be a Japanese-American from the 1920s"[1] on.

Mori did not have an easy time gaining recognition. His first collection of short stories, *Yokohama, California*, scheduled for publication in 1942, did not appear until 1949 because of the outbreak of World War II. Also, during this period, Mori, like thousands of other West Coast Japanese-Americans, was interned.[2] He spent three years in an internment camp in Topaz, Utah. While there, he helped found *Trek*, a magazine of creative writing. It took almost another thirty years before his other two major publications appeared: *The Chauvinist and Other Stories* (1979) and a novel, *Woman from Hiroshima* (1978).

In the introduction to *Yokohama, California*, William Saroyan (our author in Chapter 1) said about Mori:

> He is a natural born writer—. . . He can see. He can see *through* the material image to the real thing; through a human being to the strange, comical, melancholy truth. . . .
>
> If someone else tried to tell you about them [the Japanese of California], you would never know them. . . . They would be Japanese; in Mori's stories they are Japanese only after you know they are men and women alive. (Toshio Mori, *Yokohama, California* (Caldwell, Idaho: The Caxton Printers, Ltd., 1949), pp. 8–9)

Our story here is from this collection.[3] I believe it bears out this assessment.

---

*milieu—atmosphere.

[1] I am grateful to Stephen Y. Mori for contributing important information about his father.

[2] At the time of this printing, legislation is before Congress to *redress* or right the wrongs done to Japanese-Americans during World War II in violation of their constitutional rights.

[3] Stephen Mori indicated that the character of the woman in this story is a composite of several individuals including his grandmother, Toshio Mori's mother.

The Woman Who Makes Swell Doughnuts

swell   *sl.*, first-rate; *inf.*, "great"

There is nothing I like to do better than to go to her
house and knock on the door and when she
opens the door, to go in. It is one of the experiences
I will long remember—perhaps the only immortality
that I will ever be lucky to meet in my short
life—and when I say experience I do not mean the
actual movement, the motor of our lives. I mean by
experience the dancing of emotions before our eyes and
inside of us, the dance that is still but is the roar and the
force capable of **stirring** the earth and the people.

stirring   here, arousing

Of course, she, the woman I visit, is old and of her
youthful beauty there is little left. Her face of today is
coarse with hard water and there is no question that she
has lived her life; given birth to six children, worked
side by side with her man for forty years, working in the
fields, working in the house, caring for the grandchildren, facing the summers and winters and also the
springs and autumns, running the household that is
completely her little world. And when I came on the
scene, when I discovered her in her little house on
Seventh Street, all of her life was behind, all of her task
in this world was **tabbed**, looked into, thoroughly attended, and all that is before her in life and the world,
all that could be before her now was to sit and be
served; duty done, work done, **time clock** punched;
old-age pension or old-age security; easy chair; soft
serene hours **till death take her**. But this was not of her,
not the least bit of her.*

coarse   rough, not smooth

tabbed   identified

time clock   prints employees'
arrival and departure times on
a card

serene   calm

till death take her   until she dies

When I visit her she takes me to the coziest chair in
the living room, where are her magazines and books in
Japanese and English. "Sit down," she says. "Make
yourself comfortable. I will come back with some hot
doughnuts just out of oil."

And before I can turn a page of a magazine she is
back with a plateful of hot doughnuts. There is nothing

---

*"This was not a part of her life; it does not describe her at all."

I can do to describe her doughnuts; it is in class by itself, without words, without demonstration. It is a doughnut, just a plain doughnut just out of oil but it is different, unique. Perhaps when I am eating her doughnuts I am really eating her; I have this foolish **notion** in my head many times and whenever I catch myself doing so I say, that is not so, that is not true. Her doughnuts really taste swell, she is the best cook I have ever known, Oriental dishes or American dishes.

notion   idea, thought

I bow humbly that such a room, such a house exists 5 in my neighborhood so I may dash in and out when my spirit **wanes**, when hell is loose. I sing gratefully that such a simple and common experience becomes an event, an event of necessity and growth. It is an event that is a part of me, an addition to the elements of the earth, water, fire, and air, and I seek the day when it will become a part of everyone.

to wane   grow smaller

All her friends, old and young, call her Mama. Everybody calls her Mama. That is not new, it is logical. I suppose there is in every block of every city in America a woman who can be called Mama by her friends and the strangers meeting her. . . . But what of a woman who isn't a mama but is, and instead **of priding in** the expansion of her little world, takes her little circle, living out her days in the little circle, perhaps never to be exploited in a biography or on everybody's tongue, but enclosed, shut, excluded from world news and newsreels; just sitting, just moving, just alive, planting the plants in the fields, caring for the children and the grandchildren and baking the tastiest doughnuts this side of the next world.

of priding in   [sic] taking pride in

When I set with her I do not need to ask deep 7 questions, I do not need to know Plato* or The Sacred Books of the East or dancing. I do not need to be **on guard**. But I am on guard and **foot-loose** because the room is alive.

on guard   watchful
foot-loose   carefree

"Where are the grandchildren?" I say. "Where are Mickey, Tadao, and Yaeko?"

"They are out in the yard," she says. "I say to 9

*Plato—A Greek philosopher (427?–347 B.C.).

them, play, play hard, go out there and play hard. You will be glad later for everything you have done with all your might."

Sometimes we sit many minutes in silence. Silence does not bother her. She says silence is the most beautiful symphony, she says the air breathed in silence is sweeter and sadder. That is about all we talk of. Sometimes I sit and gaze out the window and watch the Southern Pacific trains **rumble by** and the vehicles whizz with speed. And sometimes she catches me doing this and she nods her head and I know she understands that I think the silence in the room is great, and also the roar and the dust of the outside is great, and when she is nodding I understand that she is saying that this, her little room, her little circle, is a depot, a pause, for the weary traveler, but outside, outside of her little world there is **dissonance**, hugeness of another kind, and the travel to do. So she has her little house, she bakes the grandest doughnuts, and inside of her she houses a little depot.

She is still alive, not dead in our hours, still at the old address on Seventh Street, and stopping the narrative here about her, about her most unique doughnuts, and about her personality, is the best piece of thinking I have ever done. By having her alive, by the prospect of seeing her many more times, I have many things to think and look for in the future. Most stories would end with her death, would wait till she is peacefully dead and peacefully at rest but I cannot wait that long. I think she will grow, and her hot doughnuts just out of the oil will grow with softness and touch. And I think it would be a shame to talk of her doughnuts after she is dead, after she is formless.

Instead I take today to talk of her and her wonderful doughnuts when the earth is something to her, when the people from all parts of the earth may drop in and taste the flavor, her flavor, which is in everyone's and all flavor; talk to her, sit with her, and also taste the silence of her room and the silence that is herself; and finally go away to hope and keep alive what is alive in her, on earth and in men, expressly myself.

to rumble by   move slowly, noisily

dissonance   combination of unpleasant sounds

11

EXERCISES

A. Understanding the plan—A characterization

In Chapters 3, 4, and 5, the subject matter has been autobiographical, for the authors have used themselves as subjects. In this chapter, however, Mori describes another person, one he has known well. This *character sketch* or characterization, told in the first person, is autobiographical because the author is writing from his own experience; but the focus is on the character of "the woman who makes swell doughnuts" and her *impact* or effect on the people around her and especially on the author. Would you expect Mori to organize the story in chronological or topical order? Read the story and check your expectations.

B. Vocabulary study—Degrees of formality

1. Look at the title. What adjective does Mori use to describe the doughnuts the woman makes? In standard English we would say "excellent" or "first-rate"; in informal English we might say "grand" or "great"; but "swell" is slang.

     How would the meaning differ if the title had been "The Woman Who Made First-Rate Doughnuts" rather than "The Woman Who Made Swell Doughnuts"? What does the present title suggest about the author and the woman?

2. Think about the words "mother" and "mama." One is standard and the other is informal. What are some other informal synonyms for these words? What informal synonyms do you know for the word "father"?

3. The following list of nouns, adjectives, and verbs contains pairs of words which refer to the same thing except that one word is standard and the other informal or slang. Identify these pairs and note them across from each other in the proper columns. (See Answer Key.)

     father, belly, dumb, children, boss, supervisor, dad, wealthy, stupid, kids, broke, fail, athlete, well-heeled, stomach, flunk, defeat, penniless, lick, jock

	Standard	*Informal or Slang*
	father	dad
a.	_____	_____
b.	_____	_____
c.	_____	_____
d.	_____	_____
e.	_____	_____
f.	_____	_____
g.	_____	_____
h.	_____	_____
i.	_____	_____

4. Choose three pairs of words from the list you made above. Write six sentences illustrating their use in a standard or informal context.

Example: father/dad

She said the the immigration officer, "My father is a teacher."
She said to her friends at lunch, "My dad is a teacher."

5. Brainstorming (Optional Activity): *Brainstorming* is a conference technique requiring participants to share and exchange ideas in a free and open way. The purpose of the exchange is to develop new solutions to a problem or new ways of thinking about a situation or to increase the shared knowledge of the group. The technique can sometimes be used in classrooms, too.

Set up a brainstorming session with your instructor and classmates. Make it the purpose of the session to find additional synonyms for the pairs of words in item 3 above. One person can lead the discussion. Another can write the words on the blackboard. Everyone can suggest possible words. You can also consult reference books. As one classmate suggests a word, the other class members should determine its exact meaning and degree of formality. When the group accepts a word the student at the blackboard should write it under the appropriate heading. There should be four headings in all. In addition to Standard and Informal, you can add Formal and Slang. For example,

Formal	*Standard*	*Informal*	*Slang*
male parent	father	dad, daddy pop, poppa pa	my old man

Do not stop until you have added at least 10 words to the columns. You may include idiomatic phrases.

C. Figures of speech—Metaphor and simile

A *figure of speech* is an expressive use of language which changes the usual meaning and order of words. Its purpose may be to suggest an *image* or word picture, or to describe something in a quick and sharp way by making a comparison. We can say that something is as white <u>as</u> snow or as sharp <u>as</u> a razor; or we can say that something swims <u>like</u> a fish or sings <u>like</u> a bird. This kind of comparison uses "as" or "like" and is referred to as a *simile* /ˈsim-ə-le/. Another figure of speech is called a *metaphor* /ˈmet-ə-fó(ə)r, -fər/. In this case, the wording substitutes directly for the item being compared with it. For example,

"Hong Kong is the pearl of the Orient."
"The stars are the sparkling diamonds of the night sky."

There are two strong figures of speech in Mori's story: they involve the doughnuts and the depot. Let us examine their literal and figurative uses in the story.

1. Read the references to doughnuts in the title and in paragraph 3. Are the references literal or figurative? Explain your answer.

2. Next, read the references to doughnuts in paragraphs 4, 11, and 12. What is the author comparing the doughnuts with? What similarities does he note between the two?

3. Scan the selection quickly in order to find all the words the author uses to describe the doughnuts. Divide the words into two categories: those which describe the characteristics of the doughnuts and those which give the author's opinion of them.

4. Use the information you found in item 3 above to answer these questions: How is the woman like her doughnuts? By saying that the woman is like her doughnuts, is the author using the doughnuts as a metaphor or as a simile?

5. Read paragraph 10 where the author speaks about a depot. What is the author comparing the depot to? What qualities of a depot do you think the author had in mind when he picked this word? Is "depot" being used as a metaphor or a simile? Explain your answer.

D. Structure focus—Editing—Four error types

Reviewing material to correct errors and improve expression is sometimes referred to as *editing*. In this piece, the author seems to be recording the English spoken by the people in a certain section of San Francisco. For this reason, the selection contains grammatical errors which occasionally occur in spoken English. In editing standard written English, you should correct and replace such constructions. We will look at four kinds of errors which occur in the reading.

Error Type One

Look at this sentence from paragraph 2 of the selection, noting particularly the underlined words:

"All of her task in this world was tabbed."

We have here the problem of mass versus count nouns and the singular and plural verb forms they require for agreement. In the following sentence, we can change "task" and "was" to the plural:

"All of her tasks in this world were tabbed."

Or, we can change the count noun "task" to a mass noun such as "work" to read

"All of her work in this world was tabbed."

Practice. Draw a line between possible subject and verb combinations in the following practice item. (One line has already been drawn between "all of her pie" and "was" as an example.)

All of her pie⸺ was
All of her pies   eaten.
All of her baking were

Discuss the meaning of the combinations you have indicated. Remember that "all" can act as a mass or count subject depending on what it refers to. (See Answer Key.)

Error Type Two

Here is another sentence from paragraph 2 in the reading with certain words under-lined:

> And when I <u>came</u> on the scene, when I <u>discovered</u> her in her little house on Seventh Street, all of her life <u>was</u> behind, all of her task in this world <u>was</u> tabbed, looked into, thoroughly attended, and all that <u>is</u> before her in life and the world, all that could be before her now <u>was</u> to sit and be served; duty done, work done, time clock punched; old-age pension or old-age security; easy chair; soft serene hours till death take her.

Here we have the problem of the proper sequence of tenses in certain complex sentences. At the beginning of the sentence we have the dependent time clause "And when I came on the scene. . . ." It is in the past tense. The sequence of tenses which follow must reflect this past time. One verb is in the present tense. It should be changed from "is" to "was."

Practice. Look at the following sentences. Make any changes in the main clauses that are necessary in order to keep the proper sequences of tenses. Do <u>not</u> change the "when" clauses.

a. When I came upon the scene, I found that all of the farmers had finished their work and what is waiting for them was a delicious dinner.

_____

_____

b. When I come upon the scene, I will find that all of the farmers are finishing their work and what was waiting for them is a delicious dinner.

_____

_____

Error Type Three

This sentence is from paragraph 3 in the reading.

"When I visit her she takes me to the coziest chair in the living room, <u>where are</u> her magazines and books in Japanese and English."

The problem here is one of word order. When a "WH" (information) question is changed to a dependent clause, question word order is changed to statement word order. Thus, "where are her magazines and books in Japanese and English" becomes "where her magazines and books in Japanese and English <u>are</u>." (See Appendix.)

Practice. Look at the following sentence and change the question word order of the dependent clause to a statement word order.

"Whenever I come to her house, she shows me where are her paintings and pictures of her family."

_____

_____

Error Type Four

Study this sentence from paragraph 4 in the reading.

"There is nothing I can do to describe her doughnuts; <u>it is</u> in [a] class by <u>itself</u>, without words, without demonstration."

The problem here is one of clarity of reference. The reference word or phrase must agree in number and gender with the item or items referred to. Thus, in referring to the doughnuts of the first clause, the pronoun reference in the second clause must be plural also. In the second clause, "it is" must be changed to "they are," and "itself" to "themselves."

Practice. Look at the following sentence and change the reference world or phrase to agree in number and gender with the item or items referred to.

"There is nothing I can do to describe his writing; they are in a class by itself."

_____

_____

Editing the Error Types

Study the sentences which follow. Keeping in mind the error types we have discussed, edit them where necessary. In some sentences you may find more than one error or you may find no errors. (Then check the Answer Key.)

a. Her children were grown, her work were done, her life were serene now. _____

_____

b. It is hard to describe her. They are in a class by themselves. _____

_____

c. She explained to me what are they doing. _____

_____

d. There is nothing I like to do better than to go to her house. _____

_____

e. She told me where were the grandchildren. _____

_____

f. Sometimes I sat and watched the Southern Pacific trains as they rumble by. _____

_____

E. Understanding the ideas—Questions for discussion

A basic question which comes to mind as we think about this story is why the author wanted to write about this woman. Let us come back to that question after we have considered the following:

1. In paragraph 1, the author says that experience has a special meaning for him. What does he mean by experience?

2. In paragraph 9, the woman says to her grandchildren, "You will be glad later for everything you have done with all your might." How do you interpret that statement?

3. In paragraph 10, the author considers silence. What is the *significance* or meaning and importance of silence to him? Do you think there is any relationship between the importance Mori attaches to silence and his Asian background?

4. How would you characterize the woman in terms of age, class, and education?

5. What is it that the woman creates and offers other people which the author values so highly?

F. Topics for writing

1. Describe a typical visit to the woman's house. What *usually happens* when the author goes there?

2. Write a character sketch of someone you know well and whom you admire, but who is not a member of your immediate family.* Indicate the qualities you admire in this person and try to give examples which illustrate these qualities. Give your sketch a title that suggests an important aspect or activity connected with this person. Your title may contain a metaphor or simile.

*immediate family—parents, brothers, and sisters.

3. Round Robin Composition (Optional Writing): Everyone in the class should take out a sheet of notebook paper and copy the beginning of sentence (a) below. Complete it and add another sentence. Then, pass the paper to the student to the right. This student should copy and complete the beginning of sentence (b), add another sentence, and pass the paper to the right. Do the same with sentence (c) and pass the paper along. At this point, class members should read the Round Robin compositions aloud.

   Sentence beginnings:

   a. There is nothing I like to do better than. . . .
   b. It is one of those experiences I will long remember because. . . .
   c. Instead, I take today to talk of. . . .

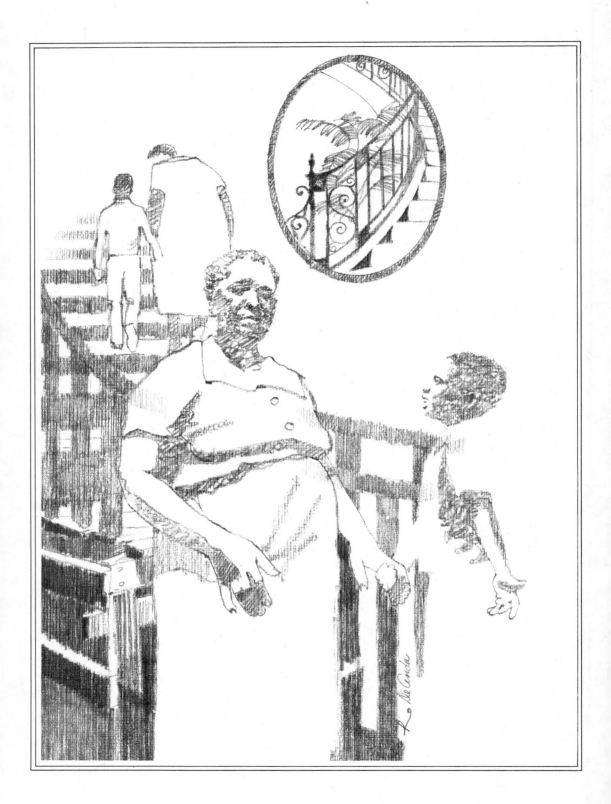

7

LANGSTON HUGHES

"Mother to Son"

from *The Weary Blues*

"Harlem"

from *Montage of a Dream Deferred*

Langston Hughes (1902–1967) was born in Missouri. By the time he was 25 he had lived in many places in the United States, gone to Mexico, travelled to Europe and parts of Asia, all the while supporting himself with odd jobs. He attended Columbia University for one year and at that time first got to know Harlem.[1] Later he went to Lincoln University and graduated from there in 1929.

Hughes was a prolific* writer. His work includes poetry, drama, fiction, essays, and autobiography. In 1926, *The Weary Blues*† was published. The first poem included here, "Mother to Son," comes from that collection. The second poem, "Harlem," comes from the collection *Montage‡ of a Dream Deferred*, published in 1951.

Hughes was a social poet. He explained the nature of his poetry well in an article called "The Negro Artist and the Racial Mountain":

> Most of my poems are racial in theme and treatment de-
> rived from the life I know. In many of them I try to grasp and
> hold some of the meanings and rhythms of jazz.
> . . . jazz to me is one of the inherent§ expressions of Negro
> life in America; the eternal tom-tom beating in the Negro
> soul—the tom-tom of revolt against weariness in a white world
> . . . the tom-tom of joy and laughter, and pain swallowed in a
> smile. (Langston Hughes, "The Negro Artist and the Racial
> Mountain," *The Nation*, 23 June, 1926, p. 693)

*prolific—extremely productive.
†blues—has come to be used in two ways: the blues can be feelings of depression or pain, or it can refer to a type of jazz which sometimes expresses these sad feelings.
‡montage—a piece of art and also of writing or music made by combining separate parts.
§inherent—inborn, innate, of its own nature.
[1]Harlem—a section of Manhattan which for the last half century has been populated largely by black people.

Mother to Son

Well, son, I'll tell you:	1
Life for me **ain't** been no crystal stair.	**ain't** *sl.*, isn't or hasn't
It's had **tacks** in it,	**tack** small, flat-headed nail with sharp point
And **splinters**,	
And boards torn up,	5 **splinter** a small, thin, sharp piece of material; a sliver
And places with no carpet on the floor—	
Bare.	
But all the time	
I'se been a-climbin' on,*	
And reachin' **landin's**,	10 **landing** platform at the top of a flight of stairs
And turnin' corners,	
And sometimes goin' in the dark	
Where there ain't been no light.	
So boy, don't you turn back.	
Don't you set down on the steps	15
'Cause you finds it's kinder hard.	
Don't you fall now—	
For I'se still goin', **honey**,	**honey** term of endearment
I'se still climbin',	
And life for me ain't been no crystal stair.	20

*Bl. Eng. dial.,
lines 9, 10	"I have been climbing on, And reaching landings,"
line 11	turnin'—turning
line 12	goin'—going
line 15	set down—sit down
line 16	"Because you find it is kind of hard."
lines 18, 19	"For I am still going, honey, I am still climbing,"

EXERCISES

A. Understanding the form—Free verse

There is a well-known poem in *regular verse* that almost every school child in the U.S. can repeat. It goes as follows:

> Roses are red
> Violets are blue
> Sugar is sweet[2]
> And so are you.

Notice that the lines are all about the same length.

1. Say the first words of the first three lines:

> roses
> violets
> sugar

Is the stress on the same syllable in all three? Do they take the same amount of time to say? These points of similarity give the three lines matching rhythm and greatest stress on the first syllable.

2. Say the first two words of the last line:

> And so

Here the stress is on the second word followed by a slight pause or slowing. This change adds the emphasis needed for a final line.

3. Notice the last words of the lines:

> red
> blue
> sweet
> you

Which ones rhyme? Are the rhyming lines paired or alternated? Regular verse can follow either pattern.

Read quickly through the poem "Mother to Son." Are the lines of approximately the same length or do they vary greatly in the number of words and syllables? Do the final words of the lines rhyme with each other either in pairs or in alternating lines? What we have here is an example of *free verse*. While the rhythm is more controlled than in ordinary prose, it is not created by lines of matching lengths. In the section Structure and Rhythm we will take a closer look at how the rhythm in this poem is constructed.

B. More about the form—Analogy and dramatic monologue

In Chapter 6, we discussed two figures of speech: simile and metaphor. We said that both involved a kind of comparison designed to give a vivid impression or description. In the poem "Mother to Son" we have another kind of comparison called an *analogy*. The purpose of an analogy, which is sometimes called an extended metaphor, is to explain a difficult subject by comparing it to a simpler, more familiar idea. For example, analogies are often made between the eye and a camera or the heart and a pump. That is, the workings of a camera or a pump are explained in terms of the ways that the eye or heart functions.

Hughes writes "Mother to Son" as a *dramatic monologue*. That is, he speaks as though he

---

[2]There are many variations for line 3.

were an actor playing the role of the mother. It is a monologue because only the mother speaks. Is it in the first person or the third person?

Read the poem again in order to understand the analogy which Hughes introduces. What is the topic under discussion? What comparison does the mother use to explain her view? What elements do the two share?

C. Structure and rhythm

1. How many sentences are in the poem? How many lines are in each sentence? With a partner, summarize the thought in lines 1 through 13 in one sentence. Summarize the thought in lines 14 through 17. Summarize the final thought in lines 17 to 20. Read the summaries aloud for class discussion. Try to reach an agreement about the meaning.

2. Look at the shortest sentence. Does its length have the effect of making the meaning stronger or weaker? Why do you think so?

3. Because the poem is a dramatic monologue, the language and rhythms are the speaker's. The mother may be talking about a very familiar staircase, or perhaps she is actually climbing one, going up ahead of her son and occasionally looking back to check on him.

A staircase such as the mother describes is typical of those built in a *tenement house*, a type of apartment house found in the poorer sections of large cities. A great number of tenements constructed in the first part of this century in New York City were six stories high because taller buildings were required to have elevators. Many tenements with their six flights of stairs were allowed to fall into disrepair.

Read the poem for information about the staircase. Actually, the mother climbs one kind of staircase and imagines another. What does she describe about the real staircase? What features does the imaginary staircase have? (Check the Answer Key.)

4. Let us look at how Hughes creates the rhythm in this poem.[3] Refer to the poem diagram on p. 80 as you read along.

   a. Several aspects of the real staircase begin with the adjective "no." The final line of the poem repeats the first phrase "no crystal stair."

   The four "no" phrases form a pattern. They are underlined in the poem diagram of "Mother to Son." Note the following phrases and line numbers. The first phrase is given.

Phrase	*Line Number*
no crystal stair	

   b. There are three other phrases which form a pattern. These phrases contain the advice that the mother gives her son. They each begin with the word "Don't." Underline them in the poem diagram. Note the phrases and their line numbers here.

---

[3]There are alternate ways of reading the lines in the poem that would create slightly different rhythm patterns. Your instructor may suggest them to you.

| | |
| Phrase | Line Number |

Don't _____   _____

_____   _____

_____   _____

c. The following pairs of phrases form different rhythm patterns. Find them in italics in the poem diagram and note their line numbers here:

| | |
| Phrase | Line Number |

  (i) tacks in it   _____

       boards torn up   _____

       [♩   ♪ ♪]

  (ii) reachin' landin's   _____

       turnin' corners   _____

       [♪ ♪ ♪ ♪]

 (iii) I'se still goin'   _____

       I'se still climbin'

       [♩ ♩ ♪ ♪]

d. A larger rhythm pattern appears in lines 3–7. We have already seen the pattern of the phrases in lines 3 and 5 (c.(i) above). We have also seen how line 6 relates to three other phrases in the poem (a. above). Now look at lines 4, 6, and 7: "splinters," line 4, has two long syllables; "no carpet on the floor," line 6, has one long, four short, and then one long syllable; finally, there is one word, "bare," line 7, with one syllable. The word "bare," as the shortest line in the poem, directs our attention to its meaning. It, together with "stair," forms the only rhyme in the poem: bare–stair.

    Here are the phrases we just discussed.

tacks in it	line 3
[♩ ♪ ♪]	
splinters	line 4
[♩ ♩]	
boards torn up	line 5
[♩ ♪ ♪]	
no carpet on the floor	line 6
[♩ ♪ ♪ ♪ ♪ ♩]	
bare	line 7
[♩]	

Read these phrases aloud while lightly tapping your foot. Can you feel the rhythm? Can you feel the way it emphasizes the meaning?

e. Look again at line 14, the shortest sentence in the poem. Every word has one syllable with one full beat. There is also a pause of one beat for the comma after the word "boy." Thus the rhythm of this line is

So boy, don't you turn back.

[♩ ♩♩ ♩ ♩ ♩ ♩]

This steady beat gives the line a special force. By this means, we feel the strength of the mother's message to her son.

Listen and tap lightly as your instructor reads the poem aloud. Then the class members should read the poem aloud while the instructor taps. A student can then read it aloud again. Try to hear how the rhythms and the meanings reinforce each other.

Mother to Son

1	(1)	Well, son, I'll tell you:
2		Life for me ain't been no crystal stair.
3	(2)	It's had *tacks in it*,
4		And splinters,
5		And *boards torn up*,
6		And places with no carpet on the floor—
7		Bare.
8	(3)	But all the time
9		I'se been a-climbin' on,
10		And *reachin' landin's*,
11		And *turnin' corners*,
12		And sometimes goin' in the dark
13		Where there ain't been no light.
14	(4)	So boy, don't you turn back.
15	(5)	Don't you set down on the steps
16		'Cause you finds it's kinder hard.
17	(6)	Don't you fall now—
18		For *I'se still goin'*, honey,
19		*I'se still climbin'*,
20		And life for me ain't been no crystal stair.

D. Vocabulary practice

1. *Endurance* and *persistence* are two qualities of the mother's character. A list of words and phrases which convey the idea of these qualities follows. Using your dictionary whenever necessary, first distinguish the difference between these two qualities. Second, mark an "E" next to those words and phrases in the list which stress the meaning of endurance; mark a "P" next to those which stress the idea of persistence. Then, give one example from the poem of the mother's endurance and one of her persistence.

Nouns	*Adjectives and Verbs*
perseverance /ˌpər-sə-ˈvir-ən(t)s/	unflagging /ˌən-ˈflag-iŋ/
steadfastness /ˈsted-ˌfas(t)-nəs/	indefatigable /ˌin-di-ˈfat-i-gə-bəl/
doggedness /ˈdȯ-gəd-nəs/	never give up
forbearance /fȯr-ˈbar-ən(t)s/	hang in
tenacity /tə-ˈnas-ət-ē/	hang on
continuance /kən-ˈtin-yə-wən(t)s/	hold on
sedulity /si-ˈd(y)ü-lət-ē/	bear
application /ˌap-lə-ˈkā-shən/	last

(Check the Answer Key.)

2. Here are two common expressions used in the United States to describe "life." What figures of speech are they?

> Life is just a bowl of cherries.
> Life is just a picnic.

Or just the opposite:

> Life is no bowl of cherries.
> Life is no picnic.

Here is a final one added from the poem:

> Life is no crystal stair.

Can you think of common expressions such as these used to describe "life" in your language?

E. Composition topics

1. Many writers in many languages have tried to explain life in terms of analogy. Common analogies of life are a river or a mountain. What are some other common analogies of life that you are familiar with? Take a comparison which you've heard before or construct an analogy which is interesting and meaningful to you. Write a paragraph in which you explain "life" in terms of this analogy. Explain the shared elements. Your paragraph may be serious or humorous.

2. Write a paragraph in which you compare the life views of the woman in the story who made swell doughnuts and the mother in the poem. Consider the following questions: (a) How do their life situations compare? (b) How does their advice to children differ? (c) How do you think they regard their own lives?

Harlem

What happens to a dream **deferred**?

deferred   postponed, delayed

Does it dry up
like a raisin in the sun?   2
Or **fester** like a **sore**—   4   **to fester**   to become infected
And then run?   **sore**   an open painful spot
Does it **stink** like **rotten** meat?   6   **to stink**   to give off an
Or **crust** and sugar over—   unpleasant smell
like a syrupy sweet?   8   **rotten**   decaying, spoiled
                   to crust   to form a dry layer
Maybe it just **sags**   **to sag**   to droop
like a heavy load.   10

Or does it explode?

EXERCISES

A. Structure and form

1. Find the answers to the following questions by reading the poem. Then fill in the blanks. The first ones have been completed as examples. (Later, check the Answer Key.)

   - How many sentences are there altogether? (List the numbers under *Sentence*: 1, 2, 3, and so on)
   - How many lines does each sentence have?
   - Are the sentences in question or statement form?
   - Are the questions in "information," "yes–no," or "or" form? (See Appendix.)
   - Which sentences rhyme and what are the rhyming words? (List line numbers and rhyming words in pairs.)

Sentence	Number of Lines	Question or Statement	Information, Yes–No, or Or Question	Rhymes
1	1	Question	Information	1: None

We can see now that the basic structure begins with a simple information question. The rest of the poem consists of possible answers to this question in the form of "yes–no" and "or" questions, a statement, and a final short "or" question ending with a strong verb.

Both the first and last lines stand separate from the rest of the poem although they remain tied to it. Line 1 stands alone as the only information question in the poem and it does not rhyme with any other line. It plays an important part by setting the topic. The last line, the short "or" question, is separated from the rest of the poem by a space and by being set in *italics*. However, the last line is tied to the rest of the poem because the final word rhymes with the final word in the preceding sentence.

2. Intonation (Optional): Listen as your instructor reads lines 2–8 aloud twice. Notice that the "or" questions beginning on lines 4 and 7 can end with rising or falling intonation. Let class members try out rising and falling intonation at the end of various sentences. Discuss the effect on meaning of these intonational patterns. For example, what is the difference in meaning of

    "What happens to a dream deferred?"

and

    "What happens to a dream deferred?"

(See Appendix for further discussion.)

B. Vocabulary—The denotation and connotation of words and phrases

We can discuss the meaning of words and phrases in terms of their *denotation* and *connotation*. *Denotation* is the precise, objective, neutral meaning that is least open to individual interpretation. *Connotation*, on the other hand, is the sum of associations, feelings, and widest range of subject elements attached to the word or phrase.

Two analogies can further explain the meaning of these two words. To understand the concept behind "connotation," consider what happens to a small pebble when you toss it into a still pond. As the pebble sinks, the water ripples out in increasingly wider circles. Think of the pebble as the initial word and the ripples as all the associated words and ideas or connotations.

To understand the idea behind "denotation," think of an arrow flying at a target. Let us say that the arrow hits the *bull's eye*, which is the central circle of the target. Think of the arrow as the initial word, and the bull's eye as the precise meaning. If the word, like the arrow, strikes the exact meaning, or the bull's eye, then you have an example of denotation.

Suppose we have the sentence "There is a moon out tonight." What elements would be contained in a denotative definition of the word "moon"? It might include a description of its appearance, the cause of such appearance, and perhaps an explanation of the fact that the moon is a satellite attracted to a planet. A connotative definition of moon might include romantic elements—beauty, light, and various emotions. A writer might select the word "moon" especially to communicate an atmosphere or a certain stage in a series of events. When Whitecloud (Chapter 5) begins his piece with the sentence "There is a moon out tonight," he associates it with the feelings and thoughts that keep him from studying.

1. Brainstorming (see Chapter 6) Activity: The class and the instructor should give as many associations and feelings as possible to each of these words:

> Harlem
> a dream
> deferred

You may consult reference books. Do not stop until you have at least five associations next to each word on the blackboard. Here are some helping questions.

Harlem

We already know that it refers to a section of New York City. Do you know the origin of the name? What ethnic groups live there? Is it associated with poverty, riches? What is it famous for—musicians, dancers, basketball players? Name some.

Dream

What happy associations does the word have? What sad ones? What is a frightening dream called? Are there absent-minded dreams, carefree ones, private and national ones? Have you ever heard of "the American dream"?

Deferred

What are some synonyms for this word? What feelings do you associate with the word—pleasure, relief, anger, frustration*? Here are some phrases to consider: "a deferred payment plan," "a deferred decision," "a deferred dream," or "a dream deferred."

2. Refer to the items that Hughes compares to the deferred dream. Describe each one in a denotative way. Here are some questions to help you.
    a. What is a raisin? What does it look like? How does it change as it is exposed to the sun? Does it become dry or moist and sticky? Does it become smaller, change color?
    b. What is a sore? What causes it to fester? Does it become dry or moist and sticky?
    c. Describe a rotting or rotten piece of meat. Compare it to fresh meat. Does it become dry or moist and sticky?
    d. Describe the appearance and taste of a sweet or candy that is *stale* or no longer fresh. Does it become dry or moist and sticky?
    e. Think of a *beast of burden*, an animal used for carrying heavy loads, or a person carrying a sagging load. What kinds of heavy loads sag—a steel box, a sack of potatoes, a bundle of wood, a bag of groceries, a barrel of beer? What makes a person or a beast sag?
    f. Describe a time bomb.

C. Classifying the ideas

Classification is a way of grouping ideas or things according to shared characteristics. You may divide the grouping and then subdivide it further into a number of categories as long as you follow a logical order. For example, you could have a main grouping or classification of biology which would include the study of all living things. You could then divide all of

---

*frustration—the feeling that comes from being prevented from doing or expressing something.

biology into two groups: botany and zoology. You could further divide botany and zoology into subgroups. For instance, you could subdivide botany into groups including seed plants, fernlike plants, mosslike plants, and thallos plants.* See the diagram:

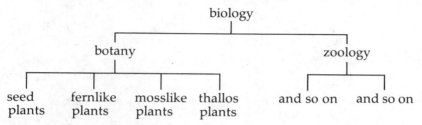

The important point is for the subgroup to really represent a subdivision of the main group. Thus, you cannot make botany the main group and biology and zoology the subgroups because this would not be logical.

Turning to the poem, let us classify the possible results of deferring a dream. Our main heading would be Possible Results of a Deferred Dream. We could divide the results into two subgroups: Decay Leading to Conditions Which Appear Unimportant, and Neglect Leading to Conditions Which Are Unpleasant, Unbearable, or Dangerous. Classify the similes and metaphor that Hughes offers under these two groups and insert them in the following diagram (refer to item B.2 above). Be prepared to explain the reasons for your choices.

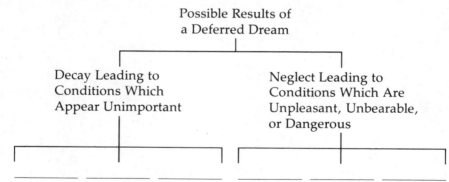

D. Topics for discussion

1. In "Mother to Son," Hughes writes in the mother's voice with her words and her feelings. Whose view is he expressing in "Harlem"? Is there more than one point of view? How would you characterize the voice in this poem which asks the opening question? Is there a different or changed voice at the end? Do you sense any warning in the last line? Who would the poet be warning? What might the warning be about?

2. In "Blue Winds Dancing" (Chapter 5), "Mother to Son," and "Harlem," a sense of injustice or unfairness is apparent. How do the reactions to the injustice differ among Whitecloud, the mother, and the narrator in "Harlem"?

*thallos plants—Latin term for plants without leaves or roots.

THE GREAT CALAMITY
OF THE AGE!

Chicago in Ashes!!

Hundreds of Millions of Dollars' Worth of Property Destroyed.

The South, the North and a Part of the West Divisions of the City in Ruins.

All The Hotels, Banks, Public Buildings, Newspaper Offices and Great Business Blocks Swept Out.

L. De Anda

8

"Morris Horowitz"

The life history of a Russian-Jewish immigrant in Chicago as recounted in the Federal Writers' Project in 1939

In this selection, we will learn about the life of a Russian-Jewish immigrant who came to the United States in the second half of the nineteenth century. This man, here given the name Morris Horowitz, settled in Chicago and made his living as a peddler* in the surrounding countryside.

Morris Horowitz was one of a number of people who told their life stories to a writer-interviewer from the Federal Writers' Project. The Federal Writers' Project (FWP) was part of the New Deal[1] program set up in the 1930s by President Franklin Roosevelt. The purpose of the Project was twofold: one, to provide a "composite portrait of America through the storytelling of people from various occupations, regions, and ethnic groups" (Ann Banks, *First-Person America* (New York: Alfred A. Knopf, Inc., 1980), p. xiv); the other, to provide relief to unemployed writers during the Great Depression.

The guided interview-writing procedure that the Federal Writers' Project followed has come to be known as the collecting of *oral history*. Today, of course, interviewers use tape recorders as well as written notes. This collecting of life histories attaches great importance "to the common man's point of view" and sees "the recounting of an individual's life history" as a "worthwhile and creative contribution to the general culture" (Tom E. Terrill and Jerrold Hirsch, eds. *Such as Us, Southern Voices of the Thirties* (Chapel Hill: Univ. of North Carolina Press, 1978), p. 295).

*peddler—a person who goes from place to place selling small goods and articles.

[1]The New Deal was the name given to the broad program instituted by Franklin D. Roosevelt to bring about an economic recovery from the Great Depression. The Great Depression followed the collapse of the stock market in 1929 and was felt internationally. It continued throughout the 1930s.

Morris Horowitz*

How did I happen to become a peddler? When I 1 came to Chicago in 1870, there was nothing else to do. I was eighteen years old. I had learned no trade in Russia. The easiest thing to do was to peddle. People coming to America today have a much harder time. There are better houses to live in and nearly everybody has a bathtub, but there are no jobs. In the old days, if you had a few dollars, you could buy some **dry goods** and peddle. But today you must know a trade or have a profession; otherwise you have no chance.

dry goods   cloth, clothing

I went to live with an aunt and uncle when I first came to Chicago. They lived in a small four-room house on Fourth Avenue. They had four children but they managed to rent one room to two roomers. I shared the bed with these two men. The day after I got to Chicago my uncle asked me if I had any money. I told him I had ten dollars. He told me to invest it in dry goods and start peddling. I peddled in Chicago until after the fire of 1871. There were not many stores, so I had no trouble selling my goods. I used to make from six to ten dollars a week. I paid my aunt three dollars a week for food and **lodging** and I saved the rest. I had the responsibility of bringing my father, two sisters, and two brothers to America.

lodging   living and sleeping space

It was the great fire of 1871 that made me a country 3 peddler. I remember the fire very well. It was in October. We used to go to bed early, because the two roomers had to go to work very early. We were getting ready to go to bed, when we heard the fire bells ringing. I asked the two men if they wanted to see where the fire was.

"Why should I care as long as our house is not on

*fictitious name—an invented name used to preserve the privacy of a real person.

fire," one of the men said. "There is a fire every Monday and Thursday in Chicago." But I wanted to see the fire, so I went out into the street. I saw the flames across the river, but I thought that since the river was between the fire and our house, there was nothing to worry about. I went back to bed. The next thing I knew my two bedfellows were shaking me. "Get up," they cried. "The whole city is on fire! Save your things! We are going to Lincoln Park."

I jumped out of bed and pulled on my pants. 5 Everybody in the house was trying to save as much as possible. I tied my clothes in a sheet. With my clothes under my arm and my pack on my back, I left the house with the rest of the family. Everybody was running north. People were carrying all kinds of crazy things. A woman was carrying a pot of soup, which was spilling all over her dress. People were carrying cats, dogs, and goats. In the great excitement people saved worthless things and left behind good things. I saw a woman carrying a big frame in which was framed her wedding veil and wreath. She said it would have been bad luck to leave it behind. . . .

No one slept that night. People gathered on the streets and all kinds of reasons were given for the fire. I stood near a minister talking to a group of men. He said the fire was sent by God as a warning that the people were **wicked**. . . . I talked to a man who lived next door   **wicked**   sinful or evil
to Mrs. O'Leary, and he told me that the fire started in Mrs. O'Leary's barn. She went out to milk the cow when it was beginning to get dark. The cow kicked the lamp over and that's how the fire started. . . .

Since many homes were burned, many people left 7 the city. Some went to live with relatives in other cities. A great many men became country peddlers. There were thousands of men walking from farm to farm with heavy packs on their backs. These peddlers carried all kinds of merchandise, things they thought farmers and their families could use.

There was no rural mail delivery in those days. The farmers very seldom saw a newspaper and were hungry for news. They were very glad to see a peddler from any large city. They wanted to hear all about the great fire. When I told a farmer that I was from Chicago, he was very glad to see me. You see, I was a newspaper and a department store.

The farms were ten, fifteen, twenty, or even thirty 9 miles apart. It would take a day sometimes to walk from one farm to the next. I used to meet peddlers from all over. It was not an easy life, but we made pretty good money. Most of the men had come from Europe and had left their families behind. We were all trying to save enough money to bring relatives to America.

The living expenses of the peddlers were very little. The farmers' wives always gave us plenty of food. I did not eat anything that was not **kosher**, but I could eat eggs and there were plenty of them. There was fresh milk and bread and butter. The farmers always gave us a place to sleep. In the summer we slept in the **hayloft**. In the winter, if there was no **spare** bed, we would sleep on the floor. When the farmer had no extra blankets, we slept with our clothes on to keep warm.

kosher   food proper to eat according to Jewish law

hayloft   upper part of a barn where hay is kept

spare   extra, not used regularly

I had a customer in Iowa and I used to get to his 11 farm once a year. He had a nice six-room house, and it was one of the few places where I could have a bed to sleep in. When I got to the place after a year's absence, there was no house. The ground was covered with snow, and I could not even see the place where the house had been. As I was looking around, thinking that I was lost, my friend the farmer came out of a dugout. I asked him what had happened to his house.

"Oh, we had a terrible storm about four months ago, and the house blew away," said the farmer. "We are living in this dugout; it isn't as nice as the house was, but it's safe and warm. Come on in."

I had never been in a dugout and I was surprised to 13 see how nice the farmer and his wife had fixed up this hole in the ground. Seven people were living in this dugout, but they made room for me. The farmers were very lonely during the long winters, and they were glad to have anybody come to their homes.

After carrying the pack on my back for two years, I decided to buy a horse and wagon. Many other peddlers got the same idea. I used to meet the small covered wagons as they drove about the country. I had now been peddling for five years and had saved enough money to bring my father, brothers, and sisters to Chicago. By that time a great many new houses had been built and we rented a four-room house on Maxwell Street. My oldest brother started peddling. One of my sisters started working in a clothing factory, while the other one kept house.

After my father had been in Chicago a few months, 15 he wanted to go to Burlington, Iowa, to see a friend who had been his neighbor in Russia. When he got there, he met this friend's daughter and decided that I ought to marry her. So I went to Burlington, met the girl, and I agreed with my father. The young lady and I were married in 1875. I rented a small house near my father's home and we furnished it. I believe we had the first rug in the neighborhood. We were very proud of our first American home. It was the beginning of a good life. I stayed home for a week with my young wife. It was my first vacation since I had come to America. Then I started off again in my wagon. During the fifty years that I peddled, I always went home for all the Jewish holidays and when a baby was born. I would stay home a week and then was off again.

Many of the men who carried packs on their backs and in covered wagons became very rich. They learned American business ways. Some of them opened small stores which their wives looked after while the men were on the road. When the stores showed a good profit, they would quit peddling. Some of the largest department stores in the country were started by men who peddled with packs on their backs.

I never got rich. My wife and I raised six children. 17 When my sisters and brothers got married, my father came to live with us. Then one of my sisters died and her children came to live with us. Then my wife brought her parents to America and they lived with us. Then we wanted our children to have an education, so we sent them to college. There never was enough money left to start any kind of business. But I feel that we made a good investment.

Hilda Polacheck, Interviewer
Federal Writers' Project
Chicago
1939

EXERCISES

A. Intensive versus extensive reading; Skimming and scanning

In studying the poems by Langston Hughes in Chapter 7 and the reading by Thomas Whitecloud in Chapter 5, we looked at the language, the form, and the ideas in great detail. We examined the way the language worked together with the form to give greater emphasis to the writer's thoughts. This study required *intensive reading*.

The selection for this chapter requires a different kind of reading. We will be looking at the material more broadly. We do not find the creative interplay of language and thought because Morris Horowitz was not a writer. The writer-interviewer who reconstructed Morris Horowitz' life story did so in accordance with these directions:

> Take down everything you hear, just as you hear it, without adding, taking away or altering* a syllable. *Your business is to record*, not correct or improve. (Benjamin A. Botkin, *Manual for Folklore Studies*, Federal Writers' Project Materials (Washington, D.C.: Archive of Folk Songs, Library of Congress, 1938).)

Therefore, you should follow an *extensive reading* approach with this selection. Read at a steady, medium pace, trying as you read to understand the general flow of Morris Horowitz' life and to follow the specific events he relates.

With this extensive approach you will be reading more quickly than you did with the intensive, puzzle-solving reading procedure you have used before. However, this broad extensive approach is not the same as *skimming* or *scanning*. The quick, surface reading you do in skimming is most suitable for determining the subject matter of the reading. In scanning, you read for certain specific bits of information or certain elements of content or organization. An example of instructions for scanning might be to "scan the reading to find out what year Morris Horowitz got married," or "scan the reading to find out which years of Morris Horowitz' life the interview covers." When you skim or scan, you may not even have to follow the author's line of thought. On the other hand, the purpose of the extensive

---

*to alter—change, modify.

reading approach is to gain an *overview* or firm impression of the whole reading. It is especially important in this selection for the reader to feel the personality of Morris Horowitz and to get the flavor of his experience.

B. Understanding the specific events

1. How did Morris Horowitz happen to become a peddler?
2. What does he remember of the Great Chicago Fire of 1871?[2]
3. What did Morris Horowitz mean when he said, "You see, I was a newspaper and a department store"?
4. How did his life in the city differ from the way he lived while peddling in the countryside?
5. What is a dugout, and how did Morris Horowitz come to sleep in one? (Refer to paragraph 11.)
6. How did he meet his wife? How did his *lifestyle* or habits and standards of living change after he got married?
7. In his comments on peddling, who, according to Morris Horowitz, were the people who became peddlers? What might be the *career path* or the successive stages in the work situation of the most successful peddlers?
8. How successful was Morris Horowitz as a peddler? What was his career path?

C. Getting an overview of Morris Horowitz' life

1. What was Morris Horowitz' attitude toward family and family obligations? How important were they to him compared to other aspects of his life? Give examples from the reading to explain your answers.
2. What was Morris Horowitz' attitude toward his work as a peddler? Did other members of his family become peddlers? Did he think that peddling would be a good occupation for other immigrants? Do you believe he wanted his children to become peddlers?
3. Here is a man looking back over his life. Does he feel that on the whole he has had a good life, or is he bitter? Is he an optimistic or pessimistic person? Is he satisfied with his life, or is he an envious person?
4. What are some of the major decisions he made in his life? Looking back upon them, is he regretful or accepting of these decisions?
5. How else would you characterize this man and his life?

---

[2]In the Great Chicago Fire of 1871, buildings in an area of about 2,000 acres (ca. 820 hectares) burned to the ground; 250 people died; 90,000 people out of a population of ca. 300,000 were left homeless. The exact cause of the fire has never been determined, but a well-known story goes that the cow of a Mrs. O'Leary knocked over a kerosene lamp in the barn which started the fire.

D. Role playing (optional activity)

Think of an older person whose life history and basic attitudes are familiar to you. This person might be a grandparent or a great aunt or uncle or someone known to you in your community or perhaps by reputation. Go over the facts of this person's life in your mind and then make a few notes.

Pretend you are this person. "Review" your life for the class. Then answer any questions the other members of the class might have.

Here is some information you might include in your "review":

- Where you have lived;
- What your occupation was, and how it developed;
- How your family situation unfolded;
- What some important choices you made were;
- How you felt about these choices when you made them, and how you feel now looking back on them;
- How you view the whole of your life now. For example, has your life been "just a bowl of cherries"; or full of "home and peace . . . and blue winds dancing over snow fields"; or has there been "no crystal stair"?

E. Topics for library research

Choose one of the following topics and consult an encyclopedia and one or two other sources for further information. Do not hesitate to approach a reference librarian for specific information about the library's holdings. Give a short oral report to the class on your findings. Two people may work on a topic together.

1. The Federal Writers' Project
2. Oral History
3. The Great Depression of 1929 and Following
4. The Growth of Chicago
5. The Great Fire of Chicago
6. Immigrant Groups in Chicago

9

EDWIN O'CONNOR

from "The 'Boy' Fragment"

Edwin O'Connor (1918–1968) was third generation Irish-American. After spending his boyhood in Woonsocket, a mill town in Rhode Island, he attended a parochial school in Providence, Rhode Island. From there he went to Notre Dame, a Catholic University in Indiana, where he majored in English literature.

The son of a medical doctor father and school teacher mother, O'Connor came from a family that was financially well off and socially well thought of. He did not personally experience the poverty and discrimination his forebears* suffered. However, he was deeply interested in the Irish-American experience.

His three major novels document this experience as it related to politics and religion. *The Last Hurrah* (1956) depicted a type of Irish urban political boss in the decades between World Wars I and II, while *All in the Family* (1966) dealt with a newer generation of Irish politicians. *The Edge of Sadness* (1961), which won a Pulitzer Prize (1962), developed a religious subject. In this novel, a priest who suffers spiritual doubt becomes an alcoholic. Later, he recovers his faith and receives a new parish. However, his experiences have reshaped his faith.

Certain character types recur in O'Connor's work. These include the "terrible old men,"[1] their cronies,† and the younger generation pulling away from tradition.

In addition, the reader finds a sense of family, a frequent confrontation‡ between characters, and a good deal of dialogue. O'Connor once said that for the earlier generation of Irish "the simple business of talking had always been the one great recreation."[2] Esther Yntema, an editor at *The Atlantic*,[3] felt that what O'Connor captured so well was "the talk—the endless, various, garrulous,§ vituperative,‖ sentimental, funny, bombastic** Irish talk." But few of O'Connor's characters are women, and he portrays those that do appear rather sketchily. "The 'Boy' Fragment" is part of a novel that O'Connor was working on when he died. Some themes from his other writings and elements from his life are evident in this selection.

---

*forebears—ancestors.
†cronies—friends, pals, buddies; companions who are allies, cohorts.
‡confrontation—dealing directly with a situation; face-to-face meeting with the opposition.
§garrulous—talkative.
‖vituperative—containing angry, attacking, abusive language.
**bombastic—containing insincere, high-sounding language.
[1]A good deal of material on O'Connor is found in the excellent Introduction to *The Best and Last of Edwin O'Connor* by Arthur Schlesinger, Jr. (Boston: Little, Brown, 1951).
[2]Daniel Aaron quotes this remark in his article in *America*, 4 May, 1968, p. 192.
[3]*The Atlantic Magazine*. Hugh Rank quotes this remark in his book *Edwin O'Connor* (Boston: Twayne Publishers, 1974), p. 59.

from The 'Boy' Fragment

[I] When I was a boy, growing up on what were 1
then the **outskirts** of the small and rather ugly
mill city where I was born, the one person I
thought about almost all the time was my father. I
worshiped him, and in a way this was strange because I
very rarely saw him. He was always away, traveling,
working—"Your father's **on the road**, dear," my mother
said—, and when he came home it was only for a few
days at a time, and as soon as the few days were over he
went away again, and then it might be weeks or a
couple of months before he came back home for another
few days.

    Whenever he went I missed him a lot, and I knew
that my mother did, too. Usually she didn't talk much
about him—usually she didn't talk much about anybody: she was mostly a quiet woman with lots of red
hair and with green eyes that could look at you for a
long time without blinking and with big smooth white
arms that were covered with **freckles**—, but every time
he went away, for a couple of days afterwards she
talked about him all the time, and in a way that made
me sure she missed him just as much as I did. . . .

[II] My grandfather, who was my mother's father—I 3
never got to meet my other grandfather, partly because
he didn't come from around here, but also because he
died when I was little—was quite a small man, but you
never knew this when you went into his drug store and
saw him sitting down on his chair in the back room.
This is where he was most of the time, because from this
chair he could look out through a peep hole in the
wall—from the front you couldn't tell the peep hole was
there unless you knew about it: it was just a tiny little
hole about as big as a dime, next to the **Castoria** bottles
and right over the **witch hazel**—to see who was coming
into the store. Then, if Fred, the other druggist who
worked for him, was busy, or if Onesime the soda clerk
hadn't come in yet, my grandfather would get down off

outskirts   edge or fringe areas

to be "on the road"   travel for work-related reasons

freckles   small, brown spots on the skin

Castoria and witch hazel   mild medicines

his chair, put on his **starched** white druggist's coat, and go out into the store to wait on the customers. When he did this you were always surprised to see how small he was standing up, because sitting down he looked like just a normal-sized man.

    Still, even though he was so small, quite a lot of people seemed to be scared of him. He had a loud voice—which might have gotten that way from talking to my grandmother, who stayed mostly at home and was deaf—, and when he said anything to you, you could tell from the way he said it he was positive he was right and that he didn't expect you to argue much with him. I never knew anybody but my mother who would **answer him back**, and that was only at special times when I heard them talking about my father. I never knew what they were saying, because even when I could hear it I couldn't understand it, but I knew that whatever it was my mother didn't like it, because all of a sudden she would say, not shouting, but fast, and interrupting whatever he was saying, "Stop it! Stop it now, Pa! And I mean right now!" And whenever she said this my grandfather would look at her for a minute, his face all mad, but he *would* stop it, and then he would start to talk about something else and in a voice that wasn't quite so loud. But this didn't happen too often, and mostly my mother would just listen and knit or do something else while my grandfather was talking about how the city wasn't as good as it used to be, or about how Father Corrigan was getting too big for his **britches**,* or about what everybody was doing that was wrong. . . .

    Usually when I went to see him in his drug store I 5 would go right in past the soda fountain and the high stools and the four white marble tables where people who didn't want to drink their sodas or eat their college ices up at the fountain could sit, and up past the boxes of chocolates and then past the cigars and the hair tonic and stuff and then in through the doorway that had the

starched crisp and stiff with laundry starch

to answer back reply rudely

britches knee pants

*getting too big for one's britches—*id.*, describes a person who acts self-important.

heavy brown curtain across it and that led into the back room. When I got in the first thing I always saw was my grandfather sitting on his chair, and I knew that he had been watching me all the way in through his peep hole.

"Hello, boy," he would say, and no matter who was there he would always hold out his cheek for me to kiss it.

"Hello, Grampa," I would say, and then I would go 7 to him and kiss him on his high bony cheek, and he would turn his head and kiss me back, and I would always smell his special smell, which was moustache and peppermints and cigarettes.

He would hold me back with his arm then and look at me and say, "How's your Ma?"

"Fine Grampa. She's fine." 9

Then he would turn to whoever else was there and say, "You all know the grandson, I think? Peg's boy?"

And usually they all did, because usually they were 11 the same people that were always there when I came in. There was Mr. Cleary, the **undertaker**, and Mr. Williams, the policeman, and Dr. Brady, who sent all his patients to my grandfather to get their prescriptions filled, and Mr. McManus, who had the hardware store and was thinking of becoming Mayor, and Mr. O'Donnell, who didn't do anything special but whose shoes were always shined very bright and who always had a new flower in his buttonhole. All of them weren't always there together, but they would come in and go out, with always a few of them there at the same time, and then there might be some men from out of the city who were salesmen—"drummers," my grandfather called them—who worked for different medicine companies and who came in to give my grandfather samples of what they were selling. . . .

[III]   One day when I went to my grandfather's drug store a little bit later than I usually did, I saw a priest I had never seen before come in, all by himself, and sit down at one of the marble tables. He was an old man, who must have been as old as my grandfather or maybe even older, except that he had lots of white hair which was parted right in the middle, and big thick eyebrows

undertaker   mortician, funeral director

which you noticed right away because they didn't match his white hair but instead were very black. He was tall and thin and walked very straight, and when he came into the drug store he didn't look anywhere but straight ahead, and went right to his table in a kind of slow marching way, one foot going right in front of the other. When he sat down he sat very straight, too, not bending or leaning on the table, and even though he didn't call over to Onesime or even look at him, almost as soon as he sat down Onesime was hurrying over to him with an ice cream soda which was so full it was spilling over the sides.

"'Ere you are, Fadder,'' he said. ''One coffee hice 13 cream soda, hextra special, jes' de way you like it!''*

And the old priest nodded at him, but without any smile at all, and said something to him that I couldn't hear, and then he began to drink his coffee ice cream soda very slowly. And after this there were lots of days when I was there that he came in after me, always by himself, and always sitting at the same table, and always with Onesime running right over to him with the extra special coffee ice cream soda. . . .

. . . one day my grandfather . . . was looking out 15 through his peep hole and all of a sudden he said, ''Back again! His Reverence!''

All the other men seemed to know who he was talking about, even though they didn't look. Mr. McManus said, ''A human tragedy, that. I thought he'd be dead by now. How old would he be, would you say, P.J.?''

''No older than me,'' my grandfather said. ''But it's 17 not a question of age, McManus. Not with him.''

'Aged in the wood,† more likely,'' Mr. Cleary said. ''Still, it's a different kind of beverage for him in here, at any rate. Is there a **clerical** discount for ice cream sodas, P.J.?''

clerical here, *adj.*, clergy and the church

''He pays,'' my grandfather said. ''I'll say that for 19 him. He pays.''

Fr. Canad. dial., ''Here you are, Father,'' he said. ''One coffee ice cream soda, extra special, just the way you like it!''
†aged in the wood—good whiskey is left for years in wooden barrels.

Dr. Brady said, "I haven't seen him in years. Professionally, that is. I suppose he's still on the best of terms with our old friend John Barleycorn?"

"Easy, easy," my grandfather said, and I saw that he was looking at me, sitting there on the steps. "Little pitchers have big ears,* gentlemen." Which was what he sometimes said when he suddenly remembered I was here and he didn't want me to hear any more of what they were talking about. When that happened he usually began to talk about something else, but I guess he must have forgotten to do that today, because he looked back through the peep hole again and after a couple of seconds he said, "At one point, some years ago, I tell you what I would have done any time I saw that man: *I would have taken my hat off to him!*"

"A brilliant man," Mr. McManus said, nodding his head and puffing on his cigar. "Our own Cardinal Newman.[4] They say he can read Latin the way you and I would read the baseball scores."

"But today," my grandfather said, going on with what he was saying, and looking at everybody, one after the other, the way he sometimes did whenever he was going to say something important, "today, you know what I'd do? *I'd keep that hat on!*"

"Oh, there's no doubt about it," Dr. Brady said. "He did wrong, very wrong."

"He did the worst thing a priest could do!" my grandfather said, his voice getting loud again. "By his behavior he gave **scandal**! And we all know what the **Gospel** says on that one: 'But who shall offend these little ones, put a millstone round his neck and drown him in the sea!' "†

scandal here, discredit to religion

Gospel Bible

"Which little ones are those, P.J.?" Mr. O'Donnell said.

"Good God Almighty, O'Donnell!" my grandfather said, and you could see he was getting mad. "It's like talking to a child, talking to you! I'm using a figure of

---

*"Little pitchers . . ."—children hear things they shouldn't.
†"But who . . ."—drown whoever causes scandal.
[4]Cardinal John Henry Newman (1801–1890), English theologian who *converted* or changed religions, going from the Church of England to the Roman Catholic Church.

speech: little ones means all of us! In general! We're all of us God's children!"

I kept looking at my grandfather, thinking of him and Mr. Cleary and Dr. Brady as little ones, when Mr. Cleary, who was at the peep hole, said, "Hello! I wouldn't be surprised if God's children weren't due for a little visit!"

"What?" my grandfather said, looking at him.   29

Mr. Cleary pointed to the peep hole. "See for yourself," he said. "His Reverence!"

My grandfather went over to the peep hole as fast   31 as he could, but even before he had a chance to look through, the brown curtain across the doorway was pushed back and there in the doorway, not coming in or going back, but just standing there, not moving, was Father Sheridan! . . .

[IV]   . . . For a minute nobody did anything, with Father Sheridan just standing where he was, still not moving, and my grandfather and his friends not moving much, either, and not saying anything. Then, suddenly, Father Sheridan took a step forward, right into the room, and looked at all the men and said, "P.J. Gentlemen. The Theology Club is still in session, I see."

He had a very deep voice, the kind of voice I didn't   33 expect him to have at all, partly because it was kind of nice to listen to. My grandfather, instead of getting mad and shouting the way I was sure he would, just said in a polite fast voice, "Good afternoon, Father." And then all the others said good afternoon Father, too, just like my grandfather, not as if they were mad at him at all, but in a funny kind of hurried-up way, as if they didn't want him to be mad at them, either.

After this nobody said anything right away, with Father Sheridan standing now in front of the doorway, not smiling, looking just the same as when he had come in, kind of still and white and **spooky**. He didn't even   **spooky**   ghostlike
seem to see me, and I was glad of that, although by now, even though I was still a little scared, I wasn't scared quite as much, because I could see that my grandfather had decided to be nice to Father Sheridan and that nothing bad would probably happen.

My grandfather coughed a little now and said,   35

"Well, Father. This is a warm day. For this time of year."

"It is warm, P.J.," Father Sheridan said, in his deep voice. "But then it is July, P.J."

After this nobody said anything at all. After an- 37 other wait Mr. Cleary all of a sudden gave his big laugh and said, "I'll tell you this much, Father: in my profession we have very few kind words to say for the month of July! July is not exactly known as your undertaker's friend!"

Mr. McManus laughed at this and said, "There's one good thing about that, Art. I'll bet ten cents you get no complaints from your clients!"

"True enough," Mr. Cleary said. "True enough. 39 You might even say that my little clients were in the nature of **silent partners**!"

Then the other men laughed at this, and I saw that they were all looking over at Father Sheridan, I guess expecting him to laugh, too. But he didn't; he didn't even smile. He just looked back at them, just the way he had since he came into the room. Then suddenly he looked away from them, and for the first time since he came in he looked right at me! I wanted to look away from him, but I couldn't, because his deep black eyes were looking at me in their steady way, and all I could do was look back at him, feeling kind of scared again and wondering what was going to happen next. But what happened was that Father Sheridan turned to my grandfather and said, "I haven't met this young man as yet."

My grandfather kind of jumped at this and said in 41 the hurried-up way, "The grandson, Father. Peg's boy. You remember Peg of course, Father? The daughter? Stand up, boy! Where are your manners!"

And he started to swing his short arms back and forth, as if he was trying to help shove me up on my feet. . . .

"This is Father Sheridan, boy. Speak up now and 43 say hello to Father."

And I would have said hello, just the way he told me to, but Father Sheridan put up his hand and said, "He's a boy, not a parrot. I'll take it for granted he can

silent partners   people who own part of a business but may not make decisions in it

say hello." Then, looking down at me, he said, "Tell me your first name."

"Joe, Father," I said. Then, I don't know why, I 45 said, "Or Joey."

"Joe. Or Joey," he said, in his deep voice. "I've seen you in here often. You like to come here, do you?"

I just nodded my head, and then he nodded his. 47 "That's understandable," he said. "The conversation of wise men is always attractive."

And then he looked around, slowly, first at my grandfather, then at all the others, almost as though he was waiting for them to say something. But I guess they didn't want to, and they didn't even seem really to be looking much at him, but more at each other instead. So after a few seconds he looked back at me and suddenly he said, "How is your father?"

And I was so surprised I didn't answer him right 49 away, not only because I didn't even know he knew my father, but also because whenever I met anybody at my grandfather's they almost never said anything about my father. They always said, "How is your mother," I suppose because she was born over here and they had known her a long time, while my father was still kind of a stranger to them. So I didn't expect it at all when Father Sheridan asked me his question, but after I got over being surprised I was glad he did, and I said, "He's fine, Father." And then I said, "Do you know my father?"

He nodded his head, just once and only a little way forward. He said, "Oh yes. I know him quite well. He's a fine man. Will you tell him that Father Sheridan was asking for him?"

I said, "Yes, Father."   51

He gave his short nod again and said, "Good boy." Then he put out his hand to me and said, "Goodbye, Joe." . . .

[V]   After he was gone everybody seemed to get mad at 53 him all over again. My grandfather ran over to the peep hole, I guess to watch Father Sheridan go out the front door. When he turned around again so that I could see him his face was all red, and the big blue vein was sticking out on his forehead, and even his thin white hairs which were usually combed out just right were now all mussed up and he looked more like a bald man than anything else. He was so mad that he could hardly talk. I never saw him so mad, and I didn't even know why.

"Only one thing in the world stood between that man and the worst **lashing** he ever got in his life!" he said, and he was really yelling. "And that is the respect I have for the Roman collar!"

lashing   here, attack with words; tongue lashing

"As well as the presence of the boy, of course," Dr. **55** Brady said. "I think all of us were thinking of that. I know I was. Otherwise . . ."

"And the presence of the boy of course!" my grandfather shouted, agreeing with him. "And don't think Father High-and-Mighty didn't count on that! Don't think for a moment he's above hiding behind a child's **knickerbockers**!"

knickerbockers   trousers that fasten just below the knees

"I almost let go on him there once myself," Mr. **57** Cleary said. "And then I said to myself, 'Don't lower yourself, Art. Don't get down to his level.'"

"I thought he got a little **sarcastic** there," Mr. O'Donnell said. "Near the end."

sarcastic   using bitter ironic language (See Exercise B)

"Oh shut up!" my grandfather said, getting mad at **59** Mr. O'Donnell now. And then, as if he suddenly remembered something, he turned to me and said, "I don't want you hanging around that man. Do you understand me?" . . .

[VI]   . . . when I finally got home, later that afternoon, I forgot all about this and all about Father Sheridan too, because I no sooner got in the front door than I smelled the cigarette smell, and I saw the suitcase at the foot of the stairs, and I ran as fast as I could up the stairs and sure enough, there on the second floor, standing in the door of my room and waiting for me, was my father!

"Hi, **buddy**!" he said, holding out both his arms to **61** me. "Back early from the office?" . . . The funny thing was that I was so excited about my father coming home that I forgot to say anything to anybody about how I met Father Sheridan. But later that night, when I was in bed and my father was in my room and had just

buddy   term of comradeship between equals; pal, partner finished telling me the newest story he had made up about Lord Crispin and Sir Chutney, I suddenly remembered, and I began to tell him about what had happened in my grandfather's drug store. When I came to Father Sheridan's name my father looked up as though I had surprised him, and when I finished he said slowly, "Well well!" He looked over at my mother who had come in while I was talking, and she looked back at him but didn't say anything. I said, "He said I should tell you he was asking for you."

"I'm glad of that," my father said. "He's a remarkable man."

"Grampa said he did something terrible," I said. 63 "He said he did the worst thing a priest could do."

"Well," my father said, "your grandfather is a remarkable man, too. In a slightly different way." Then he looked over at my mother again. "What a town," he said. "All heart." My mother still didn't say anything, but she looked kind of worried, and my father said to me, "And did Grampa tell you anything else about Father Sheridan?"

"No," I said, "except that he didn't want me to go 65 near him again."

"I see," my father said. Then he said to my mother, "I guess I must have been out of town when that rule was passed."

My mother said, "What rule?"   67

"The one called Grampa Takes Over," my father said.

My mother looked worried again and said, "Oh, 69 you know how he is. . . ."

"I do, I do," my father said. I didn't know what they were talking about, but then my father said to me, "You see, Father Sheridan's sort of a special friend of mine. I suppose that's because when your mother and I were married, he was the priest who married us."

Which was another big surprise to me. And then 71 my father told me that they were married here in Saint James Church, which was the parish we lived in, and that Father Sheridan had been the pastor of Saint James in those days.

I said, "Why isn't he the pastor now?"

My mother said now, "Because he went away."   73

"Where did he go?" I said.

"To another parish," she said. "A few miles from 75 here."

"Why did he go?" I said. "Was it a better parish than ours?"

"It's a different kind of parish from ours," she said.   77

It was a funny kind of talk, with my mother talking not the way she usually did but as though she didn't really want to talk at all. And then my father, who was sitting down at the end of my bed, suddenly **hunched himself up** nearer to me and rubbed me hard on the top of my head, the way he sometimes did. "Look," he said, "let's **clear up** a few things about Father Sheridan. First of all, he certainly didn't do the worst thing a priest could do—although exactly what that would be I don't know. Maybe arguing with your Grampa."

to hunch up   draw arms and legs close to the body

to clear up   get the facts right

"That's not fair," my mother said.   79

"I know it," my father said. "But that's all right, too. In fact," he said to me, "I don't think he even did anything so terrible at all. Unless of course he did it to you this afternoon. Did he pull a gun on you? Come at you with a knife?"

I knew of course he was only kidding, but I said, 81 "No. He didn't do anything. He was even kind of nice."

"I'll tell you why that is," my father said. "It's because he's really kind of a nice man. In fact, a very nice man. Of course even nice men can make a mistake now and then, can't they? Maybe things don't come out the way they think they will, or maybe they **get all caught up** in situations they never expected to get caught up in at all. Anyway, there they are, and sometimes they don't see how to get out. There are people like that." And he looked at my mother again. "And not only priests," he said.

to get caught up   get completely involved emotionally or intellectually

I didn't know what that meant, but I guess my 83 mother did, because even though she didn't say anything she got her worried look again, and then my father smiled a little and reached up and pulled her down so she was sitting on my bed beside him.

"So then," he said, "sometimes people like this who may not be lucky enough to have families of their own to come back to, or may not even have anybody around to talk to, sometimes they get lonely, they get tired, and sometimes . . . well, sometimes they take things that make them less lonely and tired."

"Like medicine?" I said.   85

"Like medicine," he said. "In a way. And after that they may say or do things that aren't really bad, you know, but that some other people don't expect them to say or do. And then there's usually trouble, especially if most of the other people are like somebody we know not a million miles from here."

My mother shook her head and said, "Jack . . ."   87

"Don't stop me now," he said, "just when I'm doing so well. This explanation has everything: clarity, style . . . look," he said to me, "do you understand any of this?"

"Not very much," I said. Because I really didn't 89 except that my father didn't think that Father Sheridan had done anything that was so bad after all. So I understood that much of it and he nodded his head.

"Fair enough," he said, "because that's really what I want you to understand. So that if you meet Father Sheridan again you'll know that you're meeting a nice man and you'll behave nicely towards him. You know, polite and friendly and all that."

I said, "Grampa said—"   91

"I know what Grampa said," my father said. "Now Grampa's a fine man and he buys a swell grade of chocolate syrup, but I think he probably just forgot that Father Sheridan is a friend of mine. So we'll just forget what he said to you, and if he mentions it again you can tell him I told you what to do. It may seem strange to him, but he'll get over it." . . .

[VII]   Anyway, after a while my mother had to go down- 93 stairs to see Alma* and she came up to my pillow and looked at me and then kissed me goodnight. My father said he would be down in a couple of minutes, and then my mother went out and my father said, "Move over."

---

*Alma is probably the servant.

So I did, over nearer the wall, and he lay down on the bed beside me and turned out the light. He said, "Now, let's see: we've had the prayers, haven't we?"

I said yes, because I'd said them when I came upstairs with him in the first place, but I guess he didn't remember. Then, after a minute, he said. "Now . . . any unfinished business?"

"No," I said. "I guess not. Only . . ."   95

"Only?" he said.

"Grampa might be mad at me," I said. "About 97 Father Sheridan."

"I'll tell you what I'll do," my father said. "I'll have a word with him. I don't think you'll have any trouble. Now go to sleep."

EXERCISES

A. Getting the facts of the "Boy's" world

"The 'Boy' Fragment" is fiction or, more precisely, fictitious autobiography. The author puts himself in the shoes of the young boy and lets him tell his story. The facts that make up the boy's world emerge implicitly and explicitly. Readers should approach the narrative as a detective would, always on the lookout for clues. At the same time they should note the literary skill of the writer as the stylistic points below explain.

Section I

Read these two paragraphs to see how much information the author gives about (1) where the story takes place; (2) what the nature of the father's work is; (3) what the mother looks like; (4) how she feels about her husband, and how the son detects his mother's feelings; (5) how the son regards his mother and father.

Stylistic Point. Notice the casual way O'Connor gives us this information while drawing us into the family situation.

Section II

Read the first two paragraphs to find out (1) a fact the young narrator emphasizes about the grandfather's physical appearance; (2) a fact the young boy emphasizes about his personality; (3) a description of how the grandfather runs the drugstore.

Read paragraph 3 to the end of the section to find out (4) the physical plan of the drugstore; (5) the nature of the group of men who often sit in the back of the store with the grandfather—their occupations and their common interests.

Stylistic Point. Notice that the narrator tells what he usually does and what usually happens when he goes to visit his grandfather and at the same time gives us a description of the layout of the drugstore.

Section III

Read the first three paragraphs to find out (1) what occurs the first time the boy observes the priest; (2) what the priest looks like; (3) how he moves.

Read the rest of the section to find out (4) the views that the grandfather and his cronies hold of the priest; (5) how the social position of the priest has changed over the years; (6) what good and bad qualities the group *ascribes* or assigns to the priest.

Stylistic Point. Notice that the narrator describes the first time he sees the priest (beginning with the words "One day . . ."). Next, he indicates that the same sequence occurs many times thereafter (beginning with the words "And after this there were lots of days when . . ."). The background is thus set for the <u>particular</u> day when Father Sheridan pushes the brown curtain aside to confront the group of men in the back of the store.

Section IV

Read this section to find out (1) what Father Sheridan does and says; (2) how the grandfather reacts; (3) how the cronies react; (4) how Father Sheridan brings the boy into the conversation; (5) what then *transpires* or happens between them. (Note: we will study the exact *import* or meaning of the remarks in Sections III, IV, and V in Exercise C below. The aim of the present exercise is to follow the sequence of events as closely as possible.)

Stylistic Point. Notice how infrequently the characters address each other by their real names. The men call the grandfather P.J. The grandfather refers to his daughter as Peg. This omission makes it all the more striking when the priest asks the boy his name.

Section V

Read this section to discover (1) how the mood of the group changes after the priest leaves; (2) what the new mood is; (3) how they rationalize their changed behavior; (4) what the grandfather's *stern* or strict and severe final instruction to his grandson is.

Stylistic Point. Notice how the narrator conveys the grandfather's anger. First he says that "everyone seemed to get mad" again. Then he relates that the grandfather runs to the peephole. Only when the grandfather turns does he describe the changes in his appearance. With this buildup of information, the readers are ready to believe the degree of anger the grandfather exhibits.

Section VI

Read this section to find out (1) how the boy knows his father has returned home; (2) how the father greets the son; (3) when O'Connor introduces the subject of the priest; (4) what the boy tells his parents; (5) how they react; (6) what new facts the boy learns about the priest; (7) what final instruction the father gives the son.

Stylistic Point. Notice how the writer tells the reader that the parents are communicating information to each other that the young narrator does not understand. For example, look at the exchange between the parents after Joey says that his grandfather has told him not to go near Father Sheridan again. Jack talks about his father-in-law "taking over" and Peg says, "Oh, you know how he is. . . ." The narrator writes, "I didn't know what they were talking about."

Section VII

Read this section to find out how the characters resolve the contradictory instructions that the grandfather and father give the boy.

Now that you have read the entire selection, fill in the names of the characters opposite the description of their relationship or occupation. (Then check the Answer Key.)

	Name	*Occupation or Relationship*
1.	_____	The Boy
2.	_____	The Father
3.	_____	The Mother
4.	_____	The Grandfather
5.	_____	The Priest
6.	_____	The Doctor
7.	_____	The Undertaker
8.	_____	The Policeman
9.	_____	The Hardware Store Owner
10.	_____	The Man with Shiny Shoes and a New Flower in His Buttonhole
11.	_____	The Soda Clerk
12.	_____	The Other Druggist

B. Exploring the language—The use of irony and sarcasm in the dialogue

In the introductory material we noted the special role and quality of Irish "talk." One feature of this talk is the use of verbal irony and sarcasm. All the Irish-American men in this story use it in their speech.

Verbal irony is a figure of speech in which a person says the opposite of what he or she really intends in order to make the point with greater force. If on a dark, cold, windy, rainy day one said, "What lovely weather we are having!", this would be an ironic remark. The speaker is saying just the opposite of what he or she means. The remark is intended to have a greater effect than a straight statement of facts, such as "the temperature is X degrees; the wind is blowing Y miles per hour; the rain is falling at the rate of Z inches per day." In addition, the ironic statement presupposes that the listener is aware of the actual nature of the weather.

A *sarcastic statement* is an ironic remark that is intended to be hurtful. Often, sarcasm takes the form of apparent praise, but because the meaning is exactly the opposite it is actually stinging criticism.

Turning to the reading, let us examine some of the remarks the grandfather, his cronies, Father Sheridan, and Jack make. In Section III, paragraph 4, the grandfather looks through his peephole and says, "Back again! His Reverence!" Using the most formal and respectful term of address for a priest, "His Reverence," and saying it with special force—as the exclamation point indicates—could mean one of two things. It could mean that the grandfather is referring to someone for whom he has the greatest respect, or it could mean just the opposite. The narrator continues, "All the other men seemed to know who he [P.J.] was talking about." Thus, the other men would understand which sort of reference he intended. As readers, we must see what remarks follow before we make this judgment.

Mr. McManus then says, "A human tragedy, that. I thought he'd be dead by now." Again, if you say that a person is a human tragedy, on the surface it raises his misfortune to a high level. However, if the remark is sarcastic, then it would mean that the person deserves no sympathy for his unfortunate state.

1. In the next paragraph of the same section (III), Mr. Cleary asks, "Is there a clerical discount for ice cream sodas, P.J.?" On the surface, this seems to be a simple yes–no question. But underneath is an accusation directed at the priest. What does Mr. Cleary really want to suggest? The grandfather understands. Does he agree with Mr. Cleary? Explain your answer.

2. Explain the use of irony and sarcasm in the following remarks:
   a. In paragraph 32, the first remark that Father Sheridan makes is "P.J. Gentlemen. The Theology Club is still in session, I see."
   b. Later, in paragraph 37, Mr. Cleary says, "July is not exactly known as your undertaker's friend."
   c. In paragraph 46, Father Sheridan asks the boy whether he likes to visit the drugstore. In paragraph 47, Joey nods and the priest nods, too, saying, "That's understandable. The conversation of wise men is always attractive."
   d. In paragraph 63, Joey tells his father, "Grampa said he [Father Sheridan] did something terrible. . . . He said he did the worst thing a priest could do." Explain the father's remark in paragraph 64 when after looking at his wife, he says, "What a town, . . . All heart."

3. Find another ironic or sarcastic remark in the story. Indicate the context in which the speaker makes it and whose "ears" the remark is really intended for. Then explain its double meaning.

4. Recount a situation that concludes with an ironic or sarcastic remark. Describe an actual situation you know about or make one up.

C. Vocabulary practice

1. Give synonyms for the nouns in the left-hand column by completing the words in the right-hand column. (See Answer Key.)

Example: baby   inf _____ant_____

drugstore	phar _____
gospel	Bi _____
spook	gh _____
undertaker	mor _____
crony	co _____
drummer	sal _____

2. Choose three adjectives from the list below to describe the personal qualities of each of the following characters. Then add some adjectives of your own choice to describe their physical appearance. See how closely your list corresponds with those of other class members.

The Characters

P.J.   Peg
Joey   Father Sheridan
Jack   Mr. O'Donnell

The Adjectives

respectable	self-righteous	superior
compassionate	loyal	loving
intelligent	learned /ˈlər-nəd/	stupid
warm	friendly	timid
deep	shallow	lonely
sad	vituperative /vī-ˈt(y)ü-p(ə-)rət-iv/	humorous
intimidating /in-ˈtim-i-ˌdāt-iŋ/	strong	energetic
arbitrary	hypocritical /ˌhip-ə-ˈkrit-i-kəl/	fair-minded

D. Topics for discussion and writing

1. Discuss the layout and working of the drugstore both in terms of its business and service functions and as a social meeting place. Compare it with drugstores in your country and those you have seen in the U.S. today. Describe other such gathering places that may be more typical in your country.

2. Discuss the importance of the church in the lives of this particular Irish-American group. Give some examples from the reading to illustrate your points.

3. When the grandfather appears in paragraph 4, the narrator says of him, "Still, even though he was so small, quite a lot of people seemed to be scared of him." Consider the following characters: Joey, Jack, Peg, Father Sheridan, Mr. O'Donnell. Who do you believe was scared of the grandfather and who was not? Give your view of the feelings between each of these characters and the grandfather.

4. When Father Sheridan is first introduced to the boy in Section IV, the Father asks him what his name is. The boy replies, " 'Joe, Father,' I said. Then, I don't know why, I said, 'Or Joey.' " What is the significance of this reply in terms of the personalities and feelings of the two characters?

5. When the grandfather and his cronies are discussing Father Sheridan in Section III, the grandfather says, "At one point, some years ago, I tell you what I would have done any time I saw that man: *I would have taken my hat off to him!*" Two paragraphs later he adds, "Today, do you know what I'd do? *I'd keep that hat on!*"

a. What do you suppose happened that would account for Father Sheridan's change in status? What role do you think P.J. and his cohorts, "the respectable townspeople," played?

b. Considering the conversation between Joey and his father in Section V, how do you imagine Jack behaved toward the priest and toward P.J. and his friends at the time?

c. Imagine that you are the author. Write a brief account of the events that brought Father Sheridan to his present state in the story.

10

WILLIAM MANCHESTER

"Eleanor, Portrait of an American"

from *The Glory and the Dream: A Narrative History of America, 1932–1972*

"Eleanor, Portrait of an American" is one of several biographical sketches of outstanding figures that William Manchester (b. 1922) includes in his narrative of four decades of American history, *The Glory and the Dream*. He has written full-length biographies of John F. Kennedy, *Portrait of a President* (1962), and General Douglas MacArthur, *American Caesar* (1978). He has chronicled a whole family in *A Rockefeller Family Portrait* (1959). At the moment, he is at work on a two-volume biography of Winston Churchill.

The "Eleanor" referred to here is, of course, Eleanor Roosevelt (1884–1962), cousin and wife of President Franklin D. Roosevelt (1882–1945) and niece of President Theodore Roosevelt, Jr. (1858–1919).

This *cameo* biography or biography in miniature spans the whole life of a member of the Dutch-American establishment. The term *establishment* is used to designate the group of people who have the position, power, money, and influence to set the tone of a society. Of course, in the United States almost all groups started out as immigrants, bringing another cultural heritage with them. Eleanor Roosevelt once recalled that when she was a child some of the older members of the family sometimes spoke Dutch at Sunday dinner.

In fact, Dutch settlements go right back to the beginning of the seventeenth century. When Claes Martenszen van Roosevelt arrived from Holland in the 1640s, he joined the Dutch settlement of New Amsterdam at the foot of the island of Manhattan that would later become New York City.

By the time of the American Revolution (1776–1783), the Roosevelt family was well established in the Colonies. A direct forebear of Franklin D. Roosevelt was spoken of as "Isaac the Patriot" for his services in the Revolutionary Cause. Isaac ended his career as president of New York's first bank. A direct forebear of Eleanor Roosevelt was Cornelius van Schaach Roosevelt, who, as a merchant in the building supply business, became one of the richest men in New York.

Cornelius' son (and Eleanor's grandfather), Theodore senior, devoted much of his time to civic affairs and philanthropy as well as to his business and family affairs. "At a time when most citizens of equal fortune and education were content to forget the poor and unfortunate" (Joseph P. Lash, *Eleanor and Franklin: The Story of Their Relationship Based on Eleanor Roosevelt's Private Papers* (New York: Norton, 1971), p. 5), Theodore senior, with his "troublesome conscience," as he put it, was deeply concerned with the problems of these people. His son, Theodore junior, and other relatives, including Eleanor and Franklin, followed in this tradition.

Thus, "[by] the beginning of the twentieth century, the Roosevelt family was one of the oldest and most distinguished in the U.S." (Lash, *Eleanor and Franklin*, first page of Preface). Theodore Roosevelt, Jr., sometimes referred to as "T.R." or "Teddy," was President from 1905 to 1909. Franklin D. Roosevelt (FDR) was President from 1933 to 1945. Not only was Eleanor Roosevelt First Lady; through her own work she also achieved international recognition for her service to humanity.

Eleanor, Portrait of an American

H er father was T.R.'s brother, her mother a fa- 1 mous beauty, and she was born Anna Eleanor Roosevelt in 1884. So sad, everyone said. Such an *ugly* child.

When visitors called she would hide and suck her fingers till her mother called, "Come in, Granny," explaining to the guest, "She's such a funny child, so old-fashioned that we call her Granny." And the little girl would want to sink through the floor.

Her mother died of **diphtheria** when she was eight, 3   **diphtheria**   infectious disease, her father died of alcoholism when she was nine. She   formerly often fatal was sent to live with her maternal grandmother, a strict disciplinarian. Until she was fifteen she had no friends her own age.

At eighteen she was **presented to Society**. Society   **to present to Society**   introduce **shuddered**. The girl was nearly six feet tall. Her voice   well-placed young women was loud and scratchy. Her front teeth **protruded**. She   formally wouldn't use cosmetics. She giggled at odd times.   **to shudder**   shake with fear or Sometimes she burst into tears for no apparent reason.   revulsion Her **mind was going**, the family said, and when Cousin   **to protrude**   project Franklin proposed to her, his mother Sara fought the marriage for three years.   **mind was going**   going insane

At the wedding, on March 17, 1905, Teddy **gave the** 5   **to give the bride away**   . . . to **bride away**. She had inherited his fantastic energy. Not   the bridegroom

proper in a woman, everyone **clucked**, and they disapproved of the way she spent it. Someone asked whether housekeeping bothered her. She said, "I rarely devote more than fifteen minutes a day to it." Instead she worked among the poor. And while she was out of the house in 1913, her young husband fell in love with her part-time social secretary, Lucy Mercer.

Lucy married a rich old man named Rutherfurd in 1920 and next year polio crippled Franklin. Sara wanted him to give up public life, to retire to Hyde Park as a cripple, but the doctor told Eleanor that he should return to politics; she could serve as his eyes and ears. The two women struggled. Eleanor joined the Women's Trade Union League, worked till she dropped for the Democratic party, and told Franklin that he must be governor. Sara's benevolent dictatorship* grew weaker. She wrote her brother, "Eleanor is in the lead."

He was elected governor, then President.   7

At the inaugural he arranged for a front-row seat and a private limousine for lovely Lucy Mercer-Rutherfurd.

After the inauguration Eleanor visited the second 9 encampment of the bonus marchers.† She sang songs with them, and afterward they said, "Hoover sent the army, but Roosevelt sent his wife."

The President could seldom tour the country, so his First Lady covered forty thousand miles every year, delivering lectures and visiting slums, nursery schools, playgrounds, **sharecroppers**. Franklin always questioned her closely when she returned; he **jocularly** gave her the Secret Service code name **Rover**.

"For gosh sakes," said one goggle-eyed miner to 11 another in a *New Yorker* cartoon, "here comes Mrs. Roosevelt!"

While she was away, Lucy called on the President.

In Washington, Eleanor held a press conference 13 once a week for women reporters in the Treaty Room on

a cluck noise a hen makes to call her chicks

sharecroppers tenant farmers who pay a part of their harvest as rent

jocularly jokingly

rover wanderer

*benevolent dictatorship—authoritarian rule with the good of the ruled as the goal.

†second encampment of bonus marchers—a group of veterans from World War I who were demanding certain benefits.

the second floor of the White House. Her column, *My Day*, appeared in 135 newspapers. She wrote a question-and-answer page for each issue of the *Woman's Home Companion*.* As a radio personality she was second only to Franklin. Her twice-a-week broadcasts were sponsored by Sweetheart toilet soap, Simmons mattresses, Johns-Manville building materials, Selby shoes, and Pond's cold cream; she gave all the money to the American Friends Service Committee.† Once she kept two White House receptions going at once, moving back and forth between the connecting door.

The President would meet Lucy on roads beyond Georgetown and Arlington. Once his Washington to Hyde Park train detoured to a little-used siding at Allamuchy, New Jersey, so he could visit her at her estate.

Eleanor by now knew that she could have neither romance nor a close relationship with Franklin. 15

"Back of tranquillity lies always conquered unhappiness," was her favorite quotation.

To her admirers she was mother, wife, politician, 17 stateswoman, journalist, and First Lady—all at once, and often all at the same time. She **broke more precedents** than her husband, had a greater passion for the **underdog**, and was always a little farther to the left. Once at Hyde Park she debated with Winston Churchill the best way to keep peace in the postwar world. By an Anglo-American alliance, said he; by improving living standards throughout the world, said she.

to break a precedent break with tradition

underdog weaker member

Her critics, led by Westbrook Pegler, called her a **busybody**, a **do-gooder**, a **bleeding heart**. Cartoonists drew savage caricatures of her. Anti-Eleanor jokes were cruel: "Eleanor can bite an apple through a **picket fence**." In London, Ambassador Joseph P. Kennedy‡ said she was the greatest cross he bore—"She's always sending me a note to have some little Susie Glotz§ to tea at the embassy."

busybody person who interferes in other people's affairs

do-gooder well-intentioned but ineffective social reformer

bleeding heart person who makes an over-display of pity or concern

picket fence fence made of vertical posts

*Woman's Home Companion—a women's magazine.
† American Friends Service Committee—a Quaker organization which helps those in need.
‡ Joseph P. Kennedy—President John F. Kennedy's father.
§ some little Susie Glotz—made-up name for a person of no consequence.

Once she wondered whether her **outspokenness** might be a **liability** to Franklin. (At the time she was defending the right of Americans to be Communists.) He **chuckled** and said, "Lady, it's a free country."

She was at a meeting of Washington clubwomen when word came that he had died in Warm Springs.*

In the White House she learned that Lucy had been with him at the end. She wept briefly; then, as always, she steadied herself.

Wounded by her mother, her father, her mother-in-law, and her husband, she now embraced all humanity. She continued her column, wrote fifteen books, reformed Tammany Hall,† and represented the United States at the United Nations. Year after year in the Truman and Eisenhower administrations, American women voted her the woman they most admired. Gallup‡ reported she was the most popular woman in any part of the world.

Aged seventy-four, she wrote, "We must regain a vision of ourselves as leaders of the world. We must join in an effort to use all knowledge for the good of all human beings. When we do that, we shall have nothing to fear."

Four years later she was dead. "Her glow," said Adlai Stevenson,§ had "warmed the world." The U.N. stood in silence in her honor. The three Presidents who had succeeded her husband bowed their heads as her coffin joined his in the Hyde Park garden. Over both stood a stone with an inscription she had chosen: "The only thing we have to fear is fear itself."‖

Lucy was absent. She had died in a New York City hospital fourteen years earlier.

19 **outspokenness** forthrightness
liability here, disadvantage
chuckle a quiet laugh

21

23

25

*A spa in Georgia where Roosevelt often went for treatment of his polio.
†Tammany Hall was originally a fraternal organization founded in New York City in 1789. Later, it grew into a powerful Democratic political machine.
‡The Gallup Poll gives repesentative sampling of public opinion concerning specific issues.
§Adlai Stevenson (1900–1965) was a presidential candidate and was U.S. Ambassador to the United Nations from 1960 to 1965.
‖A quotation from the first inaugural address of Franklin Roosevelt in 1933.

EXERCISES

A. Understanding Manchester's approach

A well-known expression which says "Let the facts speak for themselves" seems to apply to this selection. In this biographical sketch, we see a very lean* style of writing with no elaboration† of incidents or of details. Rather, the approach is—get the facts, get them straight, do not color them with hearsay‡ or personal opinions. Thus, this short biography is just the opposite in style of the writing in "The 'Boy' Fragment" where the assembling of background, detail, and impressions is an essential part. Just think of how much we learn about the place, people, and situation before the moment when Father Sheridan pushes aside the brown curtain.

Still, by the same token, this portrait of Eleanor Roosevelt does not compare with a computer printout. The information is not randomly presented. The arrangement of events, the clustering§ of facts, and the selection of details create its dramatic effect. The art of the writer remains; his views are implicit. The writing is all of a piece.

1. Read paragraphs 1–5 to find as many facts as you can about the following people. List these facts under the following headings:

Eleanor's father	(3 facts)
Eleanor's mother	(3 facts)
T.R.	(3 facts)
Eleanor's maternal grandmother	(2 facts)
Franklin	(3 facts)
Sara	(3 facts)
Eleanor	(5 facts)
Lucy Mercer	(2 facts)

2. True–False Quiz Activity: The class should be divided in half. One group should work on paragraphs 6–16; the other should work on paragraphs 17–25. Each group should prepare a list of *eight* True–False statements which will be used as a test for the other group. To do this, each person should make up *three* statements. Then the groups should put together the list of eight trying to cover as many facts as possible. Next, members of one group should take turns reading the statements aloud, and members of the other group should take turns answering. Then reverse roles.

B. Organization focus—Coherence: The threads that bind

We saw in A the extraordinary amount of information that Manchester packs into this short selection. We divided it into three parts, paragraphs 1–5, 6–16, and 17–25, for

---

*lean—here, including the necessary but nothing extra.
†elaboration—here, expanded discussion.
‡hearsay—gossip.
§clustering—grouping together.

convenience of study, but actually these division points were not really set by the material. Paragraph 5 concludes with the statement that "her [Eleanor's] young husband [Franklin] fell in love with her part-time social secretary, Lucy Mercer." Paragraph 6 starts with additional information about Lucy, namely that she "married a rich old man named Ruther-furd in 1920." Thus paragraphs 5 and 6 are closely bound to each other. Similarly, various other parts of this piece relate to each other; that is to say, the piece is a good example of *coherence* in writing.

Look at the following pairs of paragraphs. Indicate how the author ties them together in terms of subject matter or aspects of a topic.

1. Paragraphs 1 and 2: How does the second paragraph elaborate on a point made in the first?

2. Paragraphs 17 and 18: How do the two paragraphs combine opposite aspects of one topic?

3. Paragraphs 23 and 24: How does the second paragraph underscore the subject matter of the first?

C. Paragraph study—The effective use of short paragraphs

Paragraphs with topic sentences followed by several sentences of development are the ones students usually study. Here we have some paragraphs with only one or two sentences. As used in the piece, they are extremely effective and are examples of the "lean" writing style mentioned earlier.

Take paragraph 7. It has one sentence:

"He was elected governor, then President."

To understand this paragraph, we must see it in context with the previous one. In that context, the unwritten topic sentence might read

"What was the result of Eleanor's efforts to 'follow doctor's orders'?"

We might expand the actual sentence of the paragraph to read

"First, he was elected governor. After serving in that office, he went on to be nominated, to campaign, and to be elected President of the United States."

To further tighten the connection with the previous paragraph we might add

"Franklin accomplished all of this in opposition to his mother who wanted him to give up public life and retire to Hyde Park as a cripple."

By making these additions, we are making the connections that the writer expects us as readers to make. We are also watering down the impact of the writing. Study one of the following one-sentence paragraphs in the context of the paragraphs that precede and succeed it. Then supply a topic sentence and an explanatory one to go with it.

1. Paragraph 8: "And at the inaugural he [Franklin] arranged for a front-row seat and a private limousine for lovely Lucy Mercer Rutherfurd."

2. Paragraph 15: "Eleanor by now knew that she could have neither romance nor a close relationship with Franklin."

3. Paragraph 20: "She [Eleanor] was at a meeting of Washington clubwomen when word came that he [Franklin] had died in Warm Springs."

D. Exploring the ideas that unify the sketch

One authority on composition explains the idea of *unity* in writing by using the analogy of "a single river system . . . with all its tributaries, big or little, . . . flowing into the main stream." The central theme is the main river and "every drop of information must find its way into this theme-river. . ." (Randall E. Decker, *Patterns of Exposition 5* (Boston: Little, Brown, 1976), p. 383).

The "main river" in this piece is, of course, Eleanor. But several "tributaries" or themes wind in and out: the important women in her life; her work as a reflection of a feeling about social responsibility; Lucy; and how Eleanor conquered unhappiness. To deal with these themes, you will have to look throughout the selection because all these themes flow through the whole personality of this woman.

1. The women in Eleanor's life included her mother, her grandmother, her mother-in-law, and her husband's mistress. Note the number of times Manchester mentions these women and what effect you believe they had on Eleanor. Quote from the selection where necessary to explain your points.

2. At what important moments in Franklin's life story does the author note Lucy's presence? How does this situation affect Eleanor and how does she handle it?

3. Trace the number and nature of Eleanor's projects that are mentioned. Which relate to a sense of responsibility to her husband, to the people in her country, to the world at large? Quote the statement which gives her philosophy of social responsibility.

4. Document the *allusions* or references to the personal unhappiness that continued throughout her life. What was her favorite quotation about unhappiness?

E. Topics for discussion

1. Paragraph 22 begins, "Wounded by her mother, her father, her mother-in-law, and her husband, she now embraced all humanity." How do all these people "wound" her? Do you believe this accounts for her interest in "all humanity"?

2. How do you believe her husband, FDR, regards her? Where does she stand among the three women in his life—the other two being his mother and Lucy?

3. Even though Manchester uses a tight, factual style in presenting Eleanor's life, still his personal view of her emerges. What do you believe Manchester's evaluation is and how does he reveal it?

4. Do you think that Eleanor would have understood what the mother in the poem "Mother to Son" (Chapter 7) meant when she said,

Don't you set down on the steps
'Cause you finds its kinder hard.
Don't you fall down now—
For I'se still goin', honey,
I'se still climbin',
And life for me ain't been no crystal stair.

Could these lines describe any aspect of Eleanor's life? Explain your answer.

F. Topics for library research (optional)

Following the instructions for E in Chapter 8, choose a topic:

1. The History of Dutch Settlements in the New World
2. The Dutch Influence in New York from New Amsterdam to the Present
3. Theodore Roosevelt, Jr.
4. Franklin D. Roosevelt and the New Deal

APPENDIX OF GRAMMAR AND USAGE

Use of Present Tense to Discuss Literature (p. 9)

A number of ESL/EFL texts use various past tense forms to discuss literature or history. In this text, however, we follow the rhetorical and pedagogical convention of discussing literature, history, and so on in the present tense, which is the so-called *literary present tense*. Thus: "What does Hamlet believe in the last act?"; What does President Washington say in his first Inaugural Address?"; "What new theory of physics does Einstein propound?"

Punctuation of Direct Quotations[1] (p. 12)

Review the following examples and notice that we can place the dialogue guide just before, in the middle, or just after the quoted material.

1. He said to me, "I can't find my car."

2. "I parked it right over there," he explained.

3. "I have been gone only a short time," he continued. "What could have happened?"

4. "Was my car illegally parked?" he asked.

5. "Do you think," he asked me, "that someone stole it?"

6. "Oh, I wonder," he said looking at the No Parking sign, "if the police department has towed my car away!"

Explanation of Examples

Example 1: He said to me, "I can't find my car."

When the dialogue guide is <u>at the beginning,</u> use a comma to separate it from the quoted material. Use normal punctuation in the direct quotation and set it off with quotation marks before and after.

Example 2: "I parked it right over there," he explained.

When the dialogue guide comes <u>after</u> a quoted statement, punctuate the statement with a comma rather than the normal period; move the period to the end of the dialogue guide.

Example 3: "I have been gone only a short time," he continued. "What could have happened?"

If you add a second sentence of quoted material, retain the normal punctuation—capital letter at the beginning; period, exclamation point, or question mark at the conclusion—and set the sentence off with quotation marks before and after.

Example 4: "Was my car illegally parked?" he asked.

If a quoted question precedes the dialogue guide, then include a question mark but leave the first letter of the dialogue in lower case.

Example 5: "Do you think," he asked me, "that someone stole it?"

---

[1]For further information regarding quotation marks and direct speech, see the *Index to Modern English* by Thomas Lee Crowell, Jr. (New York: McGraw-Hill, 1964), pp. 328–332, 139–144.

If the dialogue guide comes <u>in the middle</u> of a quoted sentence, a comma ends the internal punctuation of the first part of the quoted material; the dialogue guide begins with a lower case letter and ends with a comma; and the remaining part of the quoted sentence begins with a lower case letter.

Example 6: "Oh, I wonder," he said looking at the No Parking sign, "if the police department has towed by car away!"

The punctuation described for Example 5 applies to statements as well as questions.

Some Notes about the Verb "to Tell"[2] (p. 13)

When "to tell" means "to state," typical items include

He always tells them
{
the truth.
lies, falsehoods.
a story, stories.
a joke, jokes.
the news.
the facts.
the time.
the difference between A and B.
}

When "to tell" means "to explain or describe," the word "about" typically precedes items such as

He always tells them <u>about</u>
{
the work.
experiences.
the incident.
the plans.
}

When "to tell" means "to distinguish or determine," typical items include

He can tell
{
time.
the difference between A and B.
}

Two Other Uses of the Past Future Tense[3] (p. 27)

1. The past future tense in *present unreal conditions*:

   a. If I had the money, I <u>would buy</u> a bicycle.

2. The past future tense to indicate *an action intended* to take place after a particular time in the past:

   a. I told you two days ago that I <u>would call</u> you yesterday.

   b. I told you yesterday that I <u>would write</u> you tomorrow.

Information, Yes–No, and Or Questions; "WH" Questions (pp. 71 and 82)

Information questions are associated with "WH" words and "How":

Who, Whom, What, Where, When, Why, and How.

[2]For a discussion of the difference between "to say" and "to tell," see *Mastering American English* by Rebecca E. Hayden, Dorothy W. Pilgrim, and Aurora Quiros Haggard (Englewood Cliffs, N. J.: Prentice-Hall, 1956), pp. 129–130.

[3]For an explanation of past future tense, see Crowell, *Index to Modern English*, pp. 393, 127–134.

Other words which might introduce information questions include "Whatever," "With whom," and so on.

Yes–No questions or simple questions begin with forms of the verb "to be" or with an auxiliary verb. For example,

>   Are you here?
>   Do they see?
>   Has he come?
>   Didn't she finish?
>   Can't I work?
>   Wouldn't we enjoy it?

Or questions are composed of two or more Yes–No questions joined by "or."[4] For example,

>   Will he survive or will he die?
>   Is the book blue or is it black?

Shortened version:

>   Will he survive or die?
>   Is the book blue or black?

More than two:

>   Will he survive or die or just linger on?
>   Is the book blue or black or a combination of the two?

Intonation of Information, Yes–No, and Or Questions (p. 83)

Information Questions

(a)   What happens to a dream deferred? ↘

(b)   What happens to a dream deferred? ↗

Falling intonation, as in (a), usually indicates a straightforward request for information.
Rising intonation, as in (b), suggests that the question is ironic (see *irony*, p. 112) and that the questioner does not believe there is a straightforward answer.

Yes–No Questions

The intonation of Yes–No questions may rise or fall. In either case, the Yes–No response will be expected.

Or Questions

When the intonation of an Or question rises for the first question and falls at the end of the second question, the questioner expects the responder to find one of the alternatives correct. For example,

QUESTIONER: Is this an Or question or (is it) ↗

        an Information question? ↘

---

[4]Two or more information questions can be joined by "or" but that is not a variation considered here.

RESPONDER: It is an Or question.

When the intonation of an Or question rises for both parts, then the questioner does not know whether the answer will confirm one part, both parts, or neither. For example,

QUESTIONER: Do you have any brothers or

        (do you have) any sisters?

An Or question may link more than two questions. For example,

QUESTIONER: Do you play football or

        (do you play) volleyball or

        (do you play) tennis?

If, as above, the intonation rises for the beginning part and falls at the end of the last question, then the questioner expects the responder to find one of the choices correct. But if the intonation rises for all the parts, as in the example which follows, then the questioner does not know whether any of the choices will be confirmed.

QUESTIONER: Do you play football or

        (do you play) volleyball or

        (do you play) tennis or

        (do you play) any other sport?

FOR FURTHER REFERENCE

In addition to the notations in the chapters themselves, the following materials will supply further information.

General References about Ethnic Groups

Harvard Encyclopedia of American Ethnic Groups. Ed. Stephan Thernstrom et al. Cambridge: Harvard Univ. Press, 1980.

An excellent starting point for research in this area.

Sowell, Thomas. *Ethnic America: A History.* New York: Basic Books, 1981.

An economic and social analysis of major ethnic groups.

Chapter 5

Brown, Dee. *Bury My Heart at Wounded Knee: An Indian History of the American West.* New York: Holt, Rinehart & Winston, 1971.

An American Indian history told from the Indian point of view.

Chapters 4 and 6

Aiiieeeee! An Anthology of Asian-American Writers. Ed. Frank Chin. Washington, D. C.: Howard Univ. Press, 1974.

The editor's introduction gives a picture of varied backgrounds of Asian-American writers and how their writing was accepted.

Chapter 7

Emanuel, James. *Langston Hughes.* Boston: Twayne Publishers, 1967.

A biography written by a Black poet of a generation younger than Hughes'.

Gayle, Addison. *The Black Aesthetic.* New York: Doubleday, 1971.

Gives the setting of Black artistic movements.

Hughes, Langston. *Langston Hughes Reads and Talks About His Poems.* Spoken Arts, SAC 7140-M, 1959.

Includes readings of "Mother to Son" and "Harlem."

Chapter 8

Howe, Irving. *World of Our Fathers.* New York: Harcourt Brace Jovanovich, 1976.

A social history of Jewish immigrants to the United States during the turn of the century period.

Chapter 10

Doezema, Linda P. *Dutch Americans.* Detroit: Gale Research Co., 1979.

Gives a detailed factual history.

ANSWER KEY

P. 25

(1) The teacher

(2) Joe

(3) Robert di Nella

(4) The father

(5) Giustina and Maria

P. 37

Recollection of First Day at School ___I___

The Role of Spanish ___IV___

The Schooling Process ___V___

The Process Takes Hold ___VII___

Perceptions of Spoken English ___III___

Status of Family in the Neighborhood ___II___

Closing the Gap between Home and School ___VI___

P. 48

1 "When I went to <u>kindergarten</u> . . ."

2 ". . . <u>during the three years</u> that . . ."

3 "During the <u>first silent year</u> . . ."

5 "I read aloud <u>in first grade</u> . . ."

7 "When my <u>second grade class</u> . . ."

The time span extends three years, from kindergarten through second grade.

P. 50

(a) 6   (b) 5   (c) 1   (d) 2   (e) 3   (f) 7   (g) 4

P. 67

a. father   dad

b. stomach   belly

c. stupid   dumb

d. children   kids

e. supervisor   boss

f. wealthy   well-heeled

g. penniless   broke

h. fail   flunk

i. athlete   jock

j. defeat   lick

P. 70

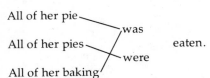

All of her pie

All of her pies

All of her baking

was

were

eaten.

"All of her pie was eaten." Meaning: Her entire pie or entire piece of pie was eaten. (There was one pie or one piece of pie altogether.)

"All of her pies were eaten." Meaning: Every pie she made or which belonged to her was eaten. (There were at least three pies altogether. If there had been two pies, then we would say "<u>Both</u> of her pies were eaten.")

"All of her baking was eaten." Meaning: Every variety of baked goods and the entire quantity she made was eaten.

P. 72

a. Her children were grown, her work <u>was</u> done, her life <u>was</u> serene now.
b. It is hard to describe her. <u>She is</u> in a class by <u>herself</u>.
c. She explained to me what they <u>were doing</u>.
d. Correct as is.
e. She told me where the grandchildren <u>were</u>.
f. Sometimes I sat and watched the Southern Pacific trains as they <u>rumbled</u> by.

P. 78

Real Staircase	*Imaginary Staircase*
tacks, splinters, boards torn up	
stairs made of wood	stairs made of crystal
bare	carpeted
dark	lighted

P. 81

E: forebearance	P: all others
continuance	
hang in	
bear	
last	

P. 82

Sentence	Number of Lines	Question or Statement	Information, Yes–No, or Or Question	Rhymes
1	1	Question	Information	None
2	2	Question	Yes-No	2 ⌠ sun
3	2	Question	Or	3 ⌡ run
4	1	Question	Yes-No	4 ⌠ meat
5	2	Question	Or	5 ⌡ sweet
6	2	Statement	—	6 ⌠ load
7	1	Question	Or	7 ⌡ explode

P. 112

1. Joe or Joey
2. Jack
3. Peg
4. P.J.
5. Father Sheridan
6. Dr. Brady
7. Mr. Cleary
8. Mr. Williams
9. Mr. McManus
10. Mr. O'Donnell
11. Onesimé
12. Fred

P. 114

drugstore   phar<u>macy</u>
gospel   <u>Bible</u>

spook   <u>ghost</u>
undertaker   <u>mortician</u>

crony   co<u>hort</u>
drummer   <u>salesman</u>

TERMS OF EXPOSITION AND CONCEPT VOCABULARY STUDIED

	Terms of Exposition	*Concept Vocabulary*
Chapter 1	characters situation narrator in the first person in the third person chronological order	to reason, rationale to rationalize, rationalization
Chapter 2	fiction non-fiction biography autobiography memoir, memoirs excerpt	first generation second generation acculturation adaptation assimilation sense of identity
Chapter 3	subtitles topic headings	a sense of alienation a sense of belonging cultural expectation
Chapter 4	topical order interpretation	explicit versus implicit culture shock
Chapter 5	interior monologue poetic license literal meaning figurative meaning repetition, parallel structure theme	animate inanimate self-condemnation
Chapter 6	characterization figure of speech simile metaphor	degrees of formality formal, standard, informal, slang brainstorming "round robin" compositions
Chapter 7	free verse dramatic monologue analogy classification	connotation denotation
Chapter 8	oral history intensive versus extensive reading skimming and scanning	lifestyle career path overview
Chapter 9	verbal irony sarcasm	cronies confrontation
Chapter 10	coherence unity	Establishment

ABBREVIATIONS USED IN THE TEXT

Foreign words and dialectic speech appear in italics and are identified as follows:

Bl. Eng. dial.   Black English dialect
Fr. Canad. dial.   French Canadian dialect
Ital.   Italian
Sicil.   Sicilian
Sp.   Spanish

Other terms:

adj.   adjective
dial.   dialect
id.   idiom
inf.   informal
pej.   pejorative
p.t.   past tense
sl.   slang

Difficult words in the explanatory text appear either in italics with an immediate explanation or in footnotes.

Footnotes which give background or explain special items are numbered successively for an entire chapter.

Footnotes which explain difficult words are marked successively for one whole page with these reference symbols:

* asterisk
† dagger
‡ double dagger
§ section symbol
‖ parallel symbol
** double asterisk

PRONUNCIATION KEY

In the *Ports of Entry* series, the pronunciation symbols follow those used in the Merriam-Webster Dictionary (College Desk Edition) with one exception. The lines enclosing the phonetic transcriptions slant to the right rather than the left. Thus we have

/   slant line used in pairs to mark the beginning and end of a transcription: /ˈpen/

ˈ   mark preceding a syllable with primary (strongest) stress: /ˈpen-mən-ˌship/

ˌ   mark preceding a syllable with secondary (next-strongest) stress: /ˈpen-mən-ˌship/

-   mark of syllable division

()   indicate that what is symbolized between is present in some utterances but not in others: *factory* /ˈfak-t(ə-)rē/

The equivalent symbols used in the *HBJ World English* series, as well as those based on the International Phonetic Alphabet (IPA), follow.

Comparative Pronunciation Symbols

Consonants

Merriam-Webster	HBJ World English	IPA Based	Key Word
p	p	p	**p**ut
b	b	b	**b**oy
t	t	t	**t**ime
d	d	d	**d**ay
k	k	k	**k**itchen
g	g	g	**g**o
ch	ch	tʃ	**ch**ild
j	j	dʒ	**j**acket
f	f	f	**f**un
v	v	v	**v**ery
th	th	θ	**th**ink
<u>th</u>	<u>th</u>	ð	**th**ese
s	s	s	**s**ir
z	z	z	**z**ero
sh	sh	ʃ	fi**sh**ing
zh	zh	ʒ	televi**s**ion
h	h	h	**h**ot
m	m	m	fa**m**ily
n	n	n	su**n**
ŋ	ŋ	ŋ	su**ng**
l	l	l	**l**et
r	r	r	**r**un
y	y	j	**y**es
w	w	w	**w**et
hw			**wh**ale

Vowels

Merriam-Webster	HBJ World English	IPA Based	Key Word
ē	i	i	m**ee**t
i	ɪ	ɪ	**i**t
e	e	e	b**e**d
a	æ	æ	b**a**d
ä	a	a	f**a**ther
ȯ	ɔ	ɔ	**au**thor
u̇	ʊ	ʊ	l**oo**k
ü	u	u	wh**o**
ər	ər	ɜ	h**er**
ə	ə	ə	c**u**p
ā	ei	eɪ	**eigh**t
ō	ou	əʊ	**o**pen
ī	ai	aɪ	**i**ce
au̇	au	aʊ	**ou**t
ȯi	ɔi	ɔɪ	b**oy**

CREDITS AND ACKOWLEDGMENTS

The author is grateful to the following publishers and copyright holders for permission to use materials reprinted in this book:

CAXTON PRINTERS, LTD. For "The Woman Who Makes Swell Doughnuts" from *Yokohama, California* by Toshio Mori. The Caxton Printers, Ltd., Caldwell, Idaho.

COLUMBIA UNIVERSITY PRESS For excerpts from *Mount Allegro: A Memoir of Italian American Life* by Jerre Mangione. Copyright © 1942, 1952, 1963, 1972 by Jerre Mangione. Reprinted with permission of the author and Columbia University Press.

GODINE PUBLISHING COMPANY For excerpt from *The Hunger of Memory: The Education of Richard Rodriguez* by Richard Rodriguez. Copyright © 1982 by Richard Rodriguez. Reprinted by permission of David R. Godine, Publisher, Boston.

HARCOURT BRACE JOVANOVICH, INC. For "The Summer of the Beautiful White Horse" by William Saroyan. Copyright 1938, 1966 by William Saroyan. Reprinted from his volume *My Name Is Aram*. For Pronunciation Key from *World English 1* by Peter Jovanovich et al., © 1980 by Harcourt Brace Jovanovich, Inc. Both reprinted by permission of the publisher.

LITTLE, BROWN & COMPANY For "Eleanor" from *The Glory and the Dream: A Narrative History of America, 1932–1972* by William Manchester. © 1973, 1974 by William Manchester. For excerpts from "The 'Boy' Fragment" from *The Best and Last of Edwin O'Connor*. Copyright 1951 by Edwin O'Connor. Both by permission of Little, Brown, and Company in association with the Atlantic Monthly Press.

HAROLD MATSON COMPANY, INC. For "Eleanor" from *The Glory and the Dream: A Narrative History of America, 1932–1972*. Copyright © 1973, 1974 by William Manchester. Reprinted by permission of the Harold Matson Company, Inc.

G. & C. MERRIAM COMPANY The system of indicating pronunciation is used by permission. From *Webster's Ninth New Collegiate Dictionary* © 1983 by Merriam-Webster, Inc., Publishers of the Merriam-Webster® Dictionaries.

NATACHEE SCOTT MOMADAY For excerpt from "Blue Winds Dancing" by Thomas S. Whitecloud from the anthology *American Indian Authors*, edited by Natachee Scott Momaday. Reprinted by permission of the editor.

WILLIAM MORRIS AGENCY For excerpt from "The 'Boy' Fragment" from *The Best and Last of Edwin O'Connor* by Edwin O'Connor. Reprinted by permission of William Morris Agency, Inc. on behalf of the author. Copyright © 1951 by Edwin O'Connor.

LAURENCE POLLINGER LIMITED For "The Summer of the Beautiful White Horse" from *My Name is Aram* by William Saroyan. Reprinted by permission of the author's agent, Laurence Pollinger Limited.

RANDOM HOUSE, INC. For excerpts from *First-Person America* by Ann Banks. Copyright © 1980 by Ann Banks. For "Harlem," copyright 1951 by Langston Hughes. Reprinted from *Selected Poems of Langston Hughes* by Langston Hughes. For "Mother to Son," copyright 1926 by Alfred A. Knopf and renewed 1954 by Langston Hughes. Reprinted from *Selected Poems of Langston Hughes* by Langston Hughes. For excerpt from *The Woman Warrior: Memoirs of a Girlhood among Ghosts* by Maxine Hong Kingston. Copyright © 1975, 1976 by Maxine Hong Kingston. All reprinted by permission of Alfred A. Knopf, Inc.

JOHN SCHAFFNER AGENCY For excerpt from *The Woman Warrior: Memoirs of a Girlhood among Ghosts* by Maxine Hong Kingston. Reprinted by permission of John Schaffner Associates, Inc. Copyright © 1976 by Maxine Hong Kingston.

GLOSSARY INDEX

The items in the Glossary Index are listed in alphabetical order. They are followed by a page number and *fn.* for footnote, *g.* for gloss, or *t.* for text.

acculturation   28 t.
acorns   57 g.
adaptations   28 t.
afire   57 g.
ahora   36 g. (*Sp.*)
ain't   76 g. (*sl.*)
alienation   34 g.
to alight   56 g.
allusions   124 t.
to alter   92 fn.
to ambush   19 g.
analogy   77 t.
to answer back   99 g.
ascribes   111 t.
assimilation   28 t.
autobiography   24 t.
babbi   23 g. (*Ital.*)
barbed wire   45 g.
barest   45 g.
bark   57 g.
bawdy ditties   24 g.
to be bent on   33 g.
to be couched in   24 g.
to be found out   6 g.
to be intimidated   33 g.
to be nuts   18 g. (*sl.*)
to be "on the road"   98 g.
to be up to   5 g.
beast of burden   84 t.
belly   3 g.
benevolent dictatorship   119 fn.
better-tempered   9 g.
bewilderment   51 fn.
birch   57 g.
bleeding heart   120 g.
blues   75 fn.
bluff   57 g.
blur   32 g.
bombastic   97 fn.
bonarma   22 g. (*Sicil.*)
borrower   13 fn.
braid   45 g.

brainstorming   68 t.
brats   33 g. (*sl.*; *pej.*)
to break a precedent   120 g.
briscola   19 g. (*Ital.*)
britches   99 g.
buddy   106 g.
bull's eye   83 t.
bungalow   33 g.
to burst   5 g.
busybody   120 g.
cameo   117 t.
capricious   4 g.
capture the flag   47 g.
career path   93 t.
Castoria and witch hazel   98 g.
characters   9 t.
character sketch   67 t.
to characterize   51 t.
check-out counter   44 g.
chipmunk   56 g.
chronological order   10 t.
chuckle   121 g.
clash   35 g.
classification   84 t.
to clear up   108 g.
clerical   101 g.
clique   22 g.
cloistered   34 g.
a cluck   119 g.
clustering   122 fn.
coarse   64 g.
coherence   123 t.
to coil   45 g.
to come to terms with   28 t.
to comply   36 g.
concentration camp   45 fn.
confrontation   97 fn.
connotation   83 t.
consoling   34 g.
conveyed   58 t.
coped   32 g.
a crazy streak   4 g.

cronies   97 fn.
crunch   57 g.
to crust   82 g.
cultural expectations   40 t. (implied by preceding paragraph)
culture   52 t.
culture shock   52 t.
curses   46 g.
to cuff   20 g.
daring   45 g.
dazed   35 g.
deferred   82 g.
defiantly   22 g.
diffident   35 g.
to deign   21 g.
denotation   83 t.
depicted   40 t.
descendant   4 fn.
diphtheria   118 g.
to dispatch   20 g.
dissonance   66 g.
ditch   5 g.
to do a stroke of hard work   22 fn.
do-gooder   120 g.
dope   19 g. (*sl.*)
double-entendre   24 g.
dramatic monologue   77 t.
dry goods   88 g.
earsplitting   20 g.
editing   69 t.
elaboration   122 fn.
endurance/persistence   81 t.
en inglés   36 g. (*Sp.*)
español   34 g. (*Sp.*)
establishment   117 t.
evolving   28 fn.
excerpt   25 t.
exotic   33 g.
expelled from   55 t.
explicit   52 t.
to exploit   61 t.

extensive reading   92 t.
facetious   11 fn.
to fester   82 g.
fiction   17 t.
fictitious   11 fn.
fictitious name   88 fn.
figure of speech   68 t.
fist   47 g.
to flunk   45 g.
foot-loose   65 g.
forebears   97 fn.
freckles   98 g.
free verse   77 t.
frowning   35 g.
frustration   84 fn.
garrulous   97 fn.
gaudy   33 g.
to get caught up   108 g.
ghetto   34 g.
ghosts   43 t.
to giggle   24 g.
to give due notice   20 g.
to give the bride away   118 g.
gob   19 g. (*sl.*)
Gospel   102 g.
to gossip   20 g.
to grasp   57 g.
gregarious   23 g.
to have a way with   5 g.
hayloft   90 g.
hearsay   122 fn.
hearty   7 g.
hind   5 g.
hinder   40 t.
to hold up the line   44 g.
honey   76 g.
to hunch up   108 g.
hysterical   57 g.
ideograph   46 g.
immediate family   72 fn.
impact   67 t.
implicit   52 t.
import   111 t.
impropriety   20 g.
inanimate   61 t.
incongruity   35 g.
inherent   75 fn.
intensive reading   92 t.
interim   23 g.

interior monologue   55 t.
interpretation   51 t.
in the first person   9 t.
in third person   9 t.
intimacy   34 g.
intricate   46 g.
intruding   35 g.
irritable   4 g.
it dawned on me   6 g.
it would surely cost him a
    scolding   21 fn.
jocularly   119 g.
to kick around   22 g.
knickerbockers   106 g.
knoll   56 g.
kosher   90 g.
lacquered   35 g.
la miseria   22 g. (*Ital.*)
landing   76 g.
to lapse into   23 g.
lashing   106 g.
lean   122 fn.
lender   13 fn.
let alone steal   3 g.
liability   121 g.
licked   57 g. (*inf.*)
lifestyle   93 t.
limbs   56 g.
lingering   24 g.
literal/figurative meanings
    59 fn.
lodging   88 g.
longings   2 g.
loon   56 g.
los americanos   33 g. (*Sp.*)
to lose track of   20 g.
to loosen the hold   34 g.
los gringos   32 g. (*Sp.*)
los otros   40 t. (*Sp.*)
maelstrom   57 g.
make-up   40 t.
maliditta terra   22 g. (*Sicil.*)
Manitou   58 g.
memoir(s)   24 t.
metaphor   68 t.
milieu   63 t.
to mind   23 g.
mind was going   118 g.
mis hermanos   34 g. (*Sp.*)

mock-urgent   35 g.
montage   75 fn.
mournful   24 g.
mute   47 g.
narrator   9 t.
non-fiction   17 t.
notion   65 g.
nun   32 fn.
oats, alfalfa   6 g.
to observe the amenities
    23 fn.
of priding in [sic]   65 g.
of their own accord   44 g.
on guard   65 g.
oral history   87 t.
outskirts   98 g.
outspokenness   121 g.
overview   93 t.
palm   56 g.
parochial schools   31 fn.
partridge   56 g.
peddler   87 fn.
to peek   46 g.
peering   57 g.
persistence   81 t.
Phi Beta Kappa   55 fn.
picket fence   120 g.
to piece together   35 g.
pine   56 g.
pious   3 g.
Plato   65 fn.
poetic license   58 t.
poker   19 g.
poverty-stricken   2 g.
to present to society   118 g.
procrastination   20 g.
prolific   75 fn.
to protrude   118 g.
pun   24 g.
to ramble   21 g.
rationale   14 t.
rationalization   14 t.
to rationalize   14 t.
to reason   14 t.
recollections   48 t.
to redress   63 fn.
regular verse   76 t.
Renaissance   31 fn.
to reprimand   21 g.

reservations   55 fn.
revelry   24 g.
rhythm/stress/pitch (notations used)   49 t.
to risk   20 g.
ritual   20 g.
to roar   4 g.
rotten   82 g.
rover   119 g.
to rumble by   66 g.
rustling   35 g.
to sag   82 g.
sarcastic   106 g.
sarcastic statement   113 t.
scan   48, 92 t.
scandal   102 g.
to scoff   18 g.
self-condemnation   60 t.
self-disgust   51 fn.
sense of alienation   39 t.
sense of belonging   39 t.
sense of identity   28 t.
sentence fragments   58 t.
serene   64 g.
to settle their accounts   20 g.
sharecroppers   119 g.
shocked   24 g.
shriek   20 g.
to shudder   118 g.
to shush her   24 g.
Siciliano   19 g. (*Ital.*)
to sigh   7 g.
significance   72 t.
silent partners   104 g.
simile   68 t.
sipping   7 g.
sirinata   23 g. (*Sicil.*)
situation   9 t.
skimming   92 t.
to skitter   44 g.
to slam   7 g.

to slide   56 g.
to snap   23 g.
snort   5 g.
snuff   21 g.
solemnly   24 g.
sore   82 g.
spare   90 g.
special dispensation   21 fn.
special-issue stamps   44 fn.
spelling bee   46 g.
splinter   76 g.
to spit   7 g.
spooky   103 g.
spun   18 g. (*p.t.*)
squeaking   44 g.
stale   84 t.
to stalk out   7 g.
starched   99 g.
to stare at   3 g.
to steer clear of   20 g.
stern   111 t.
to stink   82 g.
stirring   64 g.
straining   35 g.
stray   32 g.
streaks   56 g.
strokes   46 g.
subtitles   36 t.
surging   35 g.
surrey   7 g.
to swallow that   18 g.
to swear   8 g.
swell   64 g.
tabbed   64 g.
tack   76 g.
tact   36 g.
to take advantage of   3 g.
to take hold   36 g.
to talk back   47 g.
teak   47 g.
teeming   35 g.

telling   33 g.
tenement house   78 t.
terms of endearment   24 fn.
thallos plants   85 fn.
theme   60 t.
thief   3 g.
tic-tac-toe   45 fn.
till death take her   64 g.
time clock   64 g.
time span   48 t.
too much to resist   24 g.
topic headings   36 t.
topical order   48 t.
tracks   56 g.
trail   56 g.
transpires   111 t.
trapeze   1 fn.
tribe   4 g.
to trot   4 g.
twin   8 g.
twirling   35 g.
to tuck   19 g.
underdog   120 g.
undertaker   100 g.
unity (in writing)   124 t.
uproarious crescendo   23 g.
vagrant   4 g.
vehement   22 g.
venison   56 g.
verbal irony   112 t.
vibrant   1 fn.
vituperative   97 fn.
to wane   65 g.
warrior   43 t.
wedge   56 g.
wicked   89 g.
to wince   44 g.
to worship   57 g.
Zui   21 g. (*Sicil.*)